Target
Get back on track

AQA GCSE (9-1)
English Language
Reading

David Grant

Contents

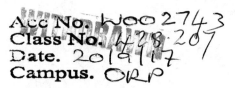

① Tackling an unseen text

This unit will help you tackle the unseen texts that you will encounter in your exams. The skills you will build are to:

- question the text before reading
- think about the whole text after reading
- consider different readings of the text.

In the exam, you will face a question like the one below. This is about the text on page 2. At the end of the unit, you will write your own response to this question.

The three key questions in the **skills boosts** will help you tackle an unseen text.

① How do I question the text before and while reading it?

② How do I question the text after reading it?

③ How do I consider different readings of the text?

Read the extract on page 2, taken from the novel *I Capture the Castle* by Dodie Smith, first published in 1948. You will tackle a 20th- or 21st-century fiction extract in the Reading section of your Paper 1 exam.

As you read, remember the following:

Before reading the extract, carefully read any introduction provided. It is intended to help you understand where the text is taken from, why it was written and other useful background information you might need.

While reading the extract, if you lose understanding of the text, stop and re-read from the last sentence or paragraph that you clearly understood.

After reading the extract, read it again.

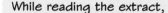

In this extract from the opening of the novel *I Capture the Castle*, 17-year-old Cassandra Mortmain describes her struggle to become a writer. She lives with her family in a decaying castle.

Source A I Capture the Castle, Dodie Smith

I write this sitting in the kitchen sink. That is, my feet are in it; the rest of me is on the draining-board, which I have padded with our dog's blanket and the tea-cosy. I can't say that I am really comfortable, and there is a depressing smell of **carbolic soap**, but this is the only part of the kitchen where there is any daylight left. And I have found that sitting in a place where you have never sat before can be inspiring. I wrote my very best poem while sitting on
5   the hen-house. Though even that isn't a very good poem. I have decided my poetry is so bad that I mustn't write any more of it.

Drips from the roof are plopping into the water-butt by the back door. The view through the windows above the sink is excessively drear. Beyond the dank garden in the courtyard are the ruined walls on the edge of the moat. Beyond the moat, the boggy ploughed fields stretch to the leaden sky. I tell myself that all the rain we have had
10   lately is good for nature, and that at any moment spring will surge on us. I try to see leaves on the trees and the courtyard filled with sunlight. Unfortunately, the more my mind's eye sees green and gold, the more drained of all colour does the twilight seem.

It is comforting to look away from the windows and towards the kitchen fire, near which my sister Rose is ironing though she obviously can't see properly, and it will be a pity if she scorches her only nightgown. (I have two, but
15   one is minus its behind.) Rose looks particularly fetching by firelight because she is a pinkish person; her skin has a pink glow and her hair is pinkish gold, very light and feathery. Although I am rather used to her I know she is a beauty. She is nearly twenty-one and very bitter with life. I am seventeen, look younger, feel older. I am no beauty but have a neatish face.

I have just remarked to Rose that our situation is really rather romantic – two girls in this strange and lonely house.
20   She replied that she saw nothing romantic about being shut up in a crumbling ruin surrounded by a sea of mud. I must admit that our home is an unreasonable place to live in. Yet I love it. The house itself was built in the time of Charles II, but it was grafted on to a fourteenth-century castle that had been damaged by Cromwell. The whole of our east wall was part of the castle; there are two round towers in it. The gatehouse is intact and a stretch of the old walls at their full height joins it to the house. And Belmotte Tower, all that remains of an even older castle, still
25   stands on its mound close by. But I won't attempt to describe our peculiar home fully until I can see more time ahead of me than I do now.

I am writing this journal partly to practise my newly acquired speed writing and partly to teach myself how to write a novel. I intend to capture all our characters and put in conversations. It ought to be good for my style to dash along without much thought, as up to now my stories have been very stiff and self-conscious. The only time
30   father obliged me by reading one of them, he said I combined stateliness with a desperate effort to be funny. He told me to relax and let the words flow out of me.

carbolic soap: a disinfectant soap with a strong odour

How do I question the text before and while reading it?

Questioning the text will help you understand and explore what you are reading and your response to it. This is perfect preparation for a high-level analysis of the text.

(1) Think about your expectations **before you read** the text and whether they were confirmed or how they changed **while you were reading** the text. Note down some ideas in the spaces below.

The characters	The events described	The ideas explored
Before reading I expected	*Before reading I expected*	*Before reading I expected*
While reading I realised	*While reading I realised*	*While reading I realised*

(2) (a) What questions occurred to you as you read the text? They might have been about the characters, events or ideas in the extract. Note down **two** of them below.

Question 1: ....

....

Question 2: ....

....

(b) Choose **one** of the questions you noted above. How might the writer have **encouraged** you to ask that question as you read the text? Write two or three sentences explaining your ideas.

....

....

....

....

(3) Look at the title of a 21st-century non-fiction text: a newspaper article published in 2016.

Social media is making us depressed: let's learn to turn it off

What expectations might you have and what questions might you ask of this text?

....

....

....

....

② How do I question the text after reading it?

After you have read the text, re-read it, thinking carefully about how the writer has written it and why.

① Read the text on page 2 again, thinking about its **structure**. Write ✐ two or three sentences to summarise how the characters, events and/or ideas in the text change and develop.

You could use sentence starters like these to help you:

| At the start of the extract... | However, when... | By the end of the extract... |

....

....

....

....

② ⓐ Note down ✐ **two** different ways in which you might expect the story to develop.

Development 1: ....

....

Development 2: ....

....

ⓑ For each idea, note down ✐ **how** the writer might have created those expectations. Is it through:

- what the characters say and do   • the ways in which the narrator tells their story
- the writer's choices of vocabulary and/or sentence structure?

....

....

....

....

ⓒ Now think about **why** the writer might have created the expectations you noted above. Was it:

- to engage the reader's interest   • to manipulate the reader's response to the characters
- to mislead the reader   • or for another reason?

Add notes ✐ to extend your ideas below.

....

....

....

....

....

....

③ How do I consider different readings of the text?

Different readers may respond very differently to the same text. During and after reading, think about how others may respond differently to you – and why.

① Look at some of the different reactions that readers have had to the setting of the story, described in source A on page 2.

A.
> The setting is presented as isolated, decaying and miserable.

B.
> The writer emphasises the potential of the setting: a crumbling house needing renovation and a beautiful setting waiting for spring.

C.
> The setting is presented as cosy and romantic: a fire burning in a castle on a cold dreary day.

a Look at the extract again. Identify at least one piece of evidence to support each of these points of view, underlining Ⓐ and labelling it ✏ A, B or C.

b Which of the three points of view above do you agree with most strongly? Write ✏ a sentence or two to explain your choice.

....

....

....

② a How might different readers respond differently to the narrator in the extract?
Write down ✏ your thoughts in the speech bubbles below.

b Write ✏ two or three sentences beneath each speech bubble, to explain why a reader might respond in this way.

Reader A
....
....
....
....
....
....
....

Reader B
....
....
....
....
....
....
....

....
....
....
....
....

Tackling an unseen text

When you tackle an unseen text you need to:

- Think about your expectations of the text based on the kind of text it is, when it was written, its title, its subject matter and any other information you are given.

- Read the text very carefully, comparing your responses to the text with your expectations.

- Think about how and why the writer might have created or manipulated your expectations of, and response to, the text.

- Think about how other readers might respond differently to the text.

Some of the questions you will face in your exams are designed to test your skill in extracting **explicit** and **implicit** information from an unseen text. Once you have read the text and explored your response, you will be ready to tackle these kinds of question.

> **explicit** clearly stated
> **implicit** implied; not clearly stated

Look at one student's response to this exam-style question.

Exam-style question

Read again the source from **lines 14 to 19**.

List **four** things from this part of the text about the narrator and her sister. **(4 marks)**

1. The narrator and her sister do not have many possessions.

2. Rose is beautiful, with pink skin and pinkish gold hair.

3. Rose is angry that she lives in a ruin in the middle of nowhere.

4. The narrator looks younger than 17 but feels older.

① Which of this student's answers are correct? Write down ✐ two or three sentences to explain your ideas.

....

....

....

....

....

....

....

....

....

....

....

Your turn!

After you have read and understood the text, identified its key points and explored the writer's intention, you are ready to tackle **all of the questions** you are likely to be asked in your exam.

Test your knowledge with the exam-style questions below.

> I write this sitting in the kitchen sink. That is, my feet are in it; the rest of me is on the draining-board, which I have padded with our dog's blanket and the tea-cosy. I can't say that I am really comfortable, and there is a depressing smell of **carbolic soap,** but this is the only part of the kitchen where there is any daylight left. And I have found that sitting in a place where you have never sat before can be inspiring.
> 5   I wrote my very best poem while sitting on the hen-house. Though even that isn't a very good poem. I have decided my poetry is so bad that I mustn't write any more of it.

Exam-style question

Read again the first part of the source, **lines 1 to 6**.

List **four** things from this part of the text about the narrator.   (4 marks)

1. ....
....
....

2. ....
....
....

3. ....
....
....

4. ....
....
....

Review your skills

Check up

Review your response to the exam-style question on page 7. Tick ✓ the column to show how well you think you have done each of the following.

	Not quite ✓	Nearly there ✓	Got it! ✓
questioned the text before and while reading it	☐	☐	☐
questioned the text after reading it	☐	☐	☐
considered different readings of the text	☐	☐	☐

Look over all of your work in this unit. Note down ✏ the three most important things to remember when you first read an unseen text.

1. ....

2. ....

3. ....

Need more practice?

Here is another exam-style question, this time relating to Source 3 on page 75: an extract from *English Journey* by J.B. Priestley. You'll find some suggested points to refer to in the Answers section.

Exam-style question

Read again the first part of **source 3, lines 1 to 12**.

Choose **four** statements below which are TRUE.

• Shade the boxes of the ones that you think are true.

• Choose a maximum of four statements.   (4 marks)

A The *Mauretania* holds the record for being the fastest ship in the world. ☐

B The *Mauretania* is a comfortable and luxurious ship. ☐

C The *Mauretania* is a very safe ship. ☐

D The *Mauretania* was launched in Jarrow. ☐

E The writer thinks that the people of Jarrow are stunted and ugly. ☐

F The writer thinks that Jarrow was poorly built. ☐

G The workers in Jarrow need a lot of food and sleep. ☐

H There are few jobs in Jarrow. ☐

How confident do you feel about each of these **skills?** Colour ✏ in the bars.

① How do I question the text before and while reading?

② How do I question the text after reading it?

③ How do I consider different readings of the text?

Select and synthesise evidence (AO1)
Explain, comment on and analyse how writers use language and structure to achieve effects and influence readers (AO2)

② Analysing a text

This unit will help you analyse a text, a skill you will need to demonstrate in **all** the longer answers you have to write in your exams. The skills you will build are to:

- identify key elements for analysis in a text
- structure your analysis
- develop your analysis.

In the exam you will face questions like the one below. This is about the text on page 10. At the end of the unit you will write your own response to this question.

This is about the text on page 10.

Exam-style question

You now need to refer **only** to **source A** (lines 20 to the end), a description of the trapper's working conditions in the mine.

How does the writer use language to make you, the reader, feel sympathy for the trapper?

(12 marks)

The three key questions in the **skills boosts** will help you analyse the text.

| ① **How do I choose what to analyse?** | ② **How do I structure my analysis?** | ③ **How do I develop my analysis?** |

Read Source A on page 10 from a government report published in 1842. You will tackle a 19th-century non-fiction extract in the Reading section of your Paper 2 exam.

As you read, remember the following: ⊘

Remember the focus of the exam question you are preparing to respond to.

Think about the ways in which the writer tries to interest and engage readers.

Underline Ⓐ or tick ⊘ any parts of the text that **you** find engaging or interesting.

In 1840, Lord Ashley persuaded parliament to set up a Royal Commission of Enquiry into Children's Employment. This extract is taken from the Royal Commission's report. It describes the life of a trapper – a child employed in coalmines to open and close the trap doors that regulated the flow of air through the mineshafts.

Source A Report of the Royal Commission of Enquiry into Children's Employment

The little trapper of eight years of age lies quiet in bed. The labours of the preceding day had **procured** sleep.

It is now between two and three in the morning and his mother shakes him, and desires him to rise, and tells him that his father has an hour ago gone off to the pit. Instantly he starts into conscious existence. He turns on his side, rubs his eyes, and gets up and comes to the blazing fire, and puts on his clothes. His coffee, such as it is,
5   stands by the side of the fire, and bread is laid down for him. The fortnight is now well advanced, the money all spent, and butter, bacon, and other luxurious accompaniments of bread, are not to be had at breakfast till next pay-day supply the means. He then fills the tin bottle with coffee, and takes a lump of bread, and sets out for the pit, into which he goes down with the cage.

He knows his place of work. It is inside one of the doors called trap-doors, for the purpose of forcing the stream
10   of air which passes in its long many-miled course from the down-shaft to the up-shaft of the pit: but which door must be opened whenever men or boys, with or without **carriages**, may wish to pass through. He seats himself in a little hole, about the size of a common fireplace, and with the string in his hand, and all his work is to pull that string when he has to open the door, and when man or boy has passed through, then to allow the door to shut of itself. Here it is his duty to sit, and be attentive, and pull his string promptly as anyone approaches. He may not
15   stir above a dozen steps with safety from his charge, lest he should be found neglecting his duty, and suffer for the same.

He sits solitary by himself and has no one to talk to him: for in the pit the whole of the people, men and boys, are as busy as if they were in a sea-fight. He however sees every now and again the pullers urging forward their trams through his gate, and derives some consolation from the glimmer of the little candle which is fixed on their trams.
20   For he himself has no light. His hours, except at such times, are passed in total darkness. For the first week of his service in the pit his father had allowed him candles to light one after another, but the expense of three-halfpence a day was so extravagant expenditure out of ten pence, the boy's daily wages, that his father of course withdrew the allowance the second week, all except one or two candles in the morning, and the week after the allowance was altogether taken away; and now except a neighbour kinder than his father now and then drop him a candle as
25   he passes, the boy has no light of his own.

Thus hour after hour passes away, but what are hours to him, seated in darkness, in the bowels of the earth? He knows nothing of the ascending or descending sun. Hunger, however, though silent and unseen, acts upon him and he betakes to his bottle of coffee and slice of bread and if desirous, he may have the luxury of softening it in a portion of the water in the pit, which is brought down for man and beast.

procured: brought
carriages: the carts used to transport coal along rails through the mine

How do I choose what to analyse?

When you begin to analyse a text, you need to identify those parts of the text which will help you to respond to the question you are answering. When you have done that, you can begin to select quotations to support your choices.

Look again at the exam-style question you are exploring:

Exam-style question

You now need to refer **only** to **source A** (lines 20 to the end), a description of the trapper's working conditions in the mine.

How does the writer use language to make you, the reader, feel sympathy for the trapper?

(12 marks)

(1) Look at some of the elements below, which writers often use to engage and manipulate the reader.

Which of these elements has the writer of the text on page 10 used to create sympathy for the trapper? Tick ✓ any that you can identify, and label 🖉 the relevant area of the extract A, B, C, etc.

A. Interesting or unusual characters, settings, ideas or facts		B. Sudden changes in character, argument, or tone		C. Dramatic events or moments of tension	

D. Twists, shocks or surprises		E. Description of a scene or situation		F. Humour	

These can be relevant to both fiction and non-fiction texts.

(2) Now look more closely at the key elements of the text you have identified. Which of the features below has the writer used in those elements? Underline Ⓐ and label 🖉 them in the extract on page 10.

a Significant structural choices
- i a non-chronological account of events
- ii a dramatic opening
- iii a surprising or shocking ending
- iv withholding then revealing significant information
- v contrasting two or more ideas, characters or events
- vi any other significant structural choices you can identify

b Significant paragraph or sentence structures
- i short, dramatic or emphatic paragraphs or sentences
- ii minor sentences (which contain no verbs)
- iii long sentences where a number of clauses build detail or atmosphere
- v sentences listing a sequence of events or ideas
- vi any other significant sentence structures you can identify

c Rich vocabulary choices
- i language with significant connotations or implications
- ii vivid, descriptive language
- iiii emotive, shocking or dramatic language
- iv persuasive or emphatic language
- v formal and/or informal language
- vi any other rich vocabulary choices you can identify

2 How do I structure my analysis?

Every point you make in an analysis should be supported with evidence from the text and analytical comment. However, following a rigid structure – such as writing in point-evidence-explanation (PEE) paragraphs – can limit the range and depth of your analysis.

Read the sentences below. They are taken from one paragraph of a student's analysis of the extract.

A. The writer emphasises the trapper's isolation throughout the second part of the extract, contrasting the trapper's solitary life with the "busy" activity of everyone else in the mine, "the whole of the people, men and boys".

B. The trapper's only "consolation" is in the "glimmer of the little candle" on the puller's trams when they pass through his gate. However, the writer says nothing about any communication between them, suggesting the trapper is as deprived of human contact as he is of light.

C. The writer introduces facts to create sympathy for the trapper's poverty: candles would cost "three halfpence a day", which is an "extravagant expenditure" as he only earns ten pence a day.

D. The writer uses a lengthy sentence to explain how, step by step, the boy's access to candles was reduced, culminating in the short final emphatic clause, "the boy has no light of his own".

E. The writer emphasises the darkness in which the boy works by making the point twice in quick succession: he "has no light" and passes his days "in total darkness".

(1) Think about the function of each of the sentences above. Some may have more than one function.

   a Write P ✎ beside any of the sentences that makes a **point**.

   b Write Q ✎ beside any of the sentences that includes a **quotation**.

   c Write A ✎ beside any of the sentences that **analyses** the text.

(2) a Which of the sentences would you include in a paragraph of analysis? Tick ✓ them.

   b How would you sequence the sentences you have ticked? Number them ✎ in your order.

   c How would you summarise the structure of the paragraph you have sequenced?
      Use 'point', 'quotation' and 'analysis' in your summary.

....

....

....

....

③ How do I develop my analysis?

To produce an effective analysis, you should aim to make your comments as detailed and specific as you can. Think about:

- commenting on the writer's choices – why the writer made them and how the writer has used them
- being precise about the impact of the writer's choices on the reader.

① Look at this quotation and comment from one student's analysis of the second paragraph of the extract on page 10.

> The writer begins the description of the trapper's working day when he gets up: "It is now between two and three in the morning and his mother shakes him, and desires him to rise, and tells him that his father has an hour ago gone off to the pit." This makes the reader feel sorry for him.

You can develop an analysis by thinking carefully about all the writer's choices. Look at the second paragraph of the extract and answer these questions to develop ideas you could add to the paragraph above.

ⓐ How does the quoted sentence's position in the paragraph add to its impact on the reader?

....

....

....

ⓑ How does the structure of this sentence add to its impact?

....

....

....

ⓒ How do the writer's vocabulary choices add to its impact?

....

....

....

ⓓ Why has the writer made these choices of paragraph, sentence structure and vocabulary?

....

....

....

....

ⓔ How does this paragraph relate to the previous section of the text?

....

....

....

....

Analysing a text

To write an effective analysis you need to do the following:

- Focus closely on the key words in the question: what are you being asked to analyse?
- Identify key elements of the text for analysis.
- Structure and develop your analysis, exploring the writer's choices and their impact on the reader.

Look at the exam-style question.

Exam-style question

You now need to refer **only** to **source A** (lines 20 to the end), a description of the trapper's working conditions in the mine.

How does the writer use language to make you, the reader, feel sympathy for the trapper?

(12 marks)

(1) Look at this paragraph from one student's response to the exam-style question above.

> The writer explains how the trapper's father gave him candles when he first worked at the mine but gradually reduced his allowance of candles until they were "altogether taken away". This makes the father sound cruel and increases the reader's sympathy for the trapper.

Think carefully about the comments you could add to the paragraph. You could use the questions on page 13 to help you. Note down ✐ some ideas below.

....

....

....

....

....

....

(2) How would you sequence the paragraph? Number ✐ your ideas above, and rewrite ✐ the paragraph below, developing the analysis as fully as possible.

....

....

....

....

....

....

....

....

Your turn!

You are now going to write ✏ your own answer in response to the exam-style question.

Exam-style question

You now need to refer **only** to **source A** (lines 20 to the end), a description of the trapper's working conditions in the mine.

How does the writer use language to make you, the reader, feel sympathy for the trapper?

(12 marks)

① Reread the final paragraph of the extract, from lines 26–29. Which ideas, event or element of the text could your paragraph of analysis focus on? Note down ✏ some possible ideas below.

....
....
....
....
....
....
....

② Which of your possible ideas would allow you to write the most developed analysis? Choose one of your ideas above and underline Ⓐ it.

③ Now think about how you will develop your analysis of the idea, event or element of the text you have chosen to focus on and note down ✏ your ideas below. Think about:

- the position of your chosen focus in the text
- how this element relates to other elements of the text
- the writer's choice of paragraph and sentence structure
- the writer's vocabulary choices
- the impact that the writer intends his choices to have on the reader.

④ How will you sequence your paragraph? Number ✏ all the ideas you noted above.

⑤ Now write ✏ one paragraph of developed analysis in response to the exam-style question on paper.

Review your skills

Check up

Review your response to the exam-style question on page 15. Tick ✓ the column to show how well you think you have done each of the following.

	Not quite ✓	Nearly there ✓	Got it! ✓
selected elements of the text for analysis	☐	☐	☐
structured my analysis	☐	☐	☐
developed my analysis	☐	☐	☐

Look over all of your work in this unit. Note down 🖊 the three most important things to remember when you analyse the text.

1. ....

2. ....

3. ....

Need more practice?

Here is another exam-style question, this time relating to source 1 on page 73: an extract from *The Secret Life of Bees* by Sue Monk Kidd. You'll find some suggested points to refer to in the Answers section.

Exam-style question

Look in detail at **lines 1 to 8** of the source.

How does the writer use language to describe the narrator's thoughts and feelings about the bees? You could include the writer's choice of:
• words and phrases
• language features and techniques
• sentence forms.

(8 marks)

How confident do you feel about each of these **skills?** Colour 🖊 in the bars.

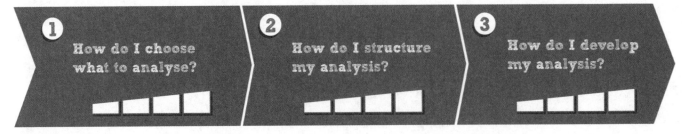

① How do I choose what to analyse?

② How do I structure my analysis?

③ How do I develop my analysis?

③ Commenting on words, phrases and language features

This unit will help you comment on a writer's use of language: the words, phrases and language features that the writer has chosen to use in a text. The skills you will build are to:

• identify and explore patterns of vocabulary choice in a text

• explore layers of meaning and a variety of responses to the writer's vocabulary choices

• identify and comment on the writer's use of tone.

In the exam you will face questions like the one below. This is about the text on page 18. This unit will prepare you to write your own response to this question, focusing on the writer's use of words, phrases and language features. Unit 4 focuses on how to analyse the writer's use of sentence forms.

Exam-style question

You now need to refer **only** to **source A** (lines 10 to the end).

How does the writer use language to describe her thoughts and feelings?

(12 marks)

The three key questions in the **skills boosts** will help you comment on language.

① How do I focus my comments on words, phrases and language features?

② How do I develop my comments on words, phrases and language features?

③ How do I comment on tone?

Read the extract on page 18 from *The Story of My Life* by Helen Keller, first published in 1903. You will tackle a 20th- or 21st-century non-fiction extract in the Reading section of your Paper 2 exam.

As you read, remember the following:

Remember the focus of the exam question you are preparing to respond to.

Think about the ways in which the writer tries to interest and engage readers and any language choices that contribute to that intention.

Underline or tick any parts of the text that **you** find significant or interesting.

Helen Keller was born in 1880. At the age of 19 months she contracted a fever that left her unable to hear, see or speak. In this extract from her autobiography, she describes how, when she was nearly seven, her teacher, Anne Sullivan, changed her life.

Source A The Story of My Life, Helen Keller

The morning after my teacher came she led me into her room and gave me a doll. When I had played with it a little while, Miss Sullivan slowly spelled into my hand the word "d-o-l-l." I was at once interested in this finger play and tried to imitate it. When I finally succeeded in making the letters correctly I was flushed with childish pleasure and pride. I did not know that I was spelling a word or even that words existed; I was simply making my fingers
5   go in monkey-like imitation. In the days that followed I learned to spell in this uncomprehending way a great many words, among them *pin*, *hat*, *cup* and a few verbs like *sit*, *stand* and *walk*. But my teacher had been with me several weeks before I understood that everything has a name.

One day, while I was playing with my new doll, Miss Sullivan put my big rag doll into my lap also, spelled "d-o-l-l" and tried to make me understand that "d-o-l-l" applied to both. Earlier in the day we had had a
10   tussle over the words "m-u-g" and "w-a-t-e-r." Miss Sullivan had tried to impress it upon me that "m-u-g" is *mug* and that "w-a-t-e-r" is *water*, but I persisted in confounding the two. In despair she had dropped the subject for the time, only to renew it at the first opportunity. I became impatient at her repeated attempts and, seizing the new doll, I dashed it upon the floor. I was keenly delighted when I felt the fragments of the broken doll at my feet. Neither sorrow nor regret followed my passionate outburst. I had not loved the doll. In the still,
15   dark world in which I lived there was no strong sentiment of tenderness. I felt my teacher sweep the fragments to one side of the hearth, and I had a sense of satisfaction that the cause of my discomfort was removed. She brought me my hat, and I knew I was going out into the warm sunshine. This thought, if a wordless sensation may be called a thought, made me hop and skip with pleasure.

We walked down the path to the **well-house**, attracted by the fragrance of the honeysuckle with which it
20   was covered. Some one was **drawing water** and my teacher placed my hand under the spout. As the cool stream gushed over one hand she spelled into the other the word water, first slowly, then rapidly. I stood still, my whole attention fixed upon the motions of her fingers. Suddenly I felt a misty consciousness as of something forgotten–a thrill of returning thought; and somehow the mystery of language was revealed to me. I knew then that "w-a-t-e-r" meant the wonderful cool something that was flowing over my hand. That living word
25   awakened my soul, gave it light, hope, joy, set it free! There were barriers still, it is true, but barriers that could in time be swept away.

I left the well-house eager to learn. Everything had a name, and each name gave birth to a new thought. As we returned to the house every object which I touched seemed to quiver with life. That was because I saw everything with the strange, new sight that had come to me. On entering the door I remembered the doll I had broken. I felt
30   my way to the hearth and picked up the pieces. I tried vainly to put them together. Then my eyes filled with tears; for I realized what I had done, and for the first time I felt repentance and sorrow.

well-house: a small building containing a water well
drawing water: pumping water from the well

1 How do I focus my comments on words, phrases and language features?

When you first consider the writer's use of language in any text, look for patterns of words or phrases that create similar or contrasting characters, situations, thoughts or feelings. You can then explore how individual vocabulary choices contribute to the impact of these patterns on the text and on the reader.

1 Which of the following pairs of ideas are presented as similar or contrasting in the text on page 18? Draw lines 🖉 to link them – then add 🖉 any of your own ideas.

The writer and her teacher	The writer's house and the outside world	
The writer's thoughts and feelings at the beginning and at the end of the text	The writer misunderstanding then understanding written language	

2 Look at some quotations from source A below. Draw 🖉 lines linking any quotations that are similar or contrasting in their ideas and/or the writer's use of language.

A. "I was keenly delighted when I felt the fragments of the broken doll at my feet. Neither sorrow nor regret followed my passionate outburst." (lines 13–14)

B. "In the still, dark world in which I lived there was no strong sentiment of tenderness." (lines 14–15)

C. "I knew I was going out into the warm sunshine. This thought … made me hop and skip with pleasure." (lines 18–19)

D. "That living word awakened my soul, gave it light, hope, joy, set it free!" (lines 24–25)

E. "every object which I touched seemed to quiver with life" (line 28)

F. "my eyes filled with tears; for I realized what I had done, and for the first time I felt repentance and sorrow." (lines 30–31)

3 Choose one pair of quotations from question 2 that you have linked. Now circle Ⓐ any of the writer's language choices in those quotations that create a similarity or a contrast.

4 Write 🖉 a sentence or two explaining why you chose the two quotations and the language choices you have circled and linked.

....

....

....

....

....

....

....

② How do I develop my comments on words, phrases and language features?

You can explore a text by considering a range of possible meanings, readings, interpretations and responses – and the ways in which the writer's use of language supports them.

① Look carefully at these sentences from the extract on page 18.

> I knew then that "w-a-t-e-r" meant the wonderful cool something that was flowing over my hand. That living word awakened my soul, gave it light, hope, joy, set it free!

a Choose **one** word or phrase from the sentences above that you feel is particularly rich in meaning. Some words have been highlighted to help you choose.

b Note down 🖉 at least **two** different ideas, connotations or implications that your chosen word or phrase suggests to you.

....

....

....

....

....

② Look carefully at this short extract from the text on page 18. Think about the different responses that the writer is trying to create.

> … seizing the new doll, I dashed it upon the floor. I was keenly delighted when I felt the fragments of the broken doll at my feet. Neither sorrow nor regret followed my passionate outburst. I had not loved the doll. In the still, dark world in which I lived there was no strong sentiment of tenderness.

a Think about ways in which the writer encourages the reader to feel **antipathy** for her behaviour in this part of the text. Circle Ⓐ any language choices that contribute to this response.

> antipathy: the opposite of sympathy – to dislike or feel hostility

b Now think about ways in which the writer encourages the reader to feel sympathy for her. Underline Ⓐ any language choices that contribute to this response.

c Why might the writer have intended to encourage both of these very different responses in the reader? Write 🖉 a sentence or two explaining your ideas.

....

....

....

....

....

3 How do I comment on tone?

The writer's language choices help to create the tone of a piece of writing: the mood the writer aims to create or the voice they use to express their ideas.

① Look at some students' comments on the tone that the writer creates at different points in the text on page 18.

A. The writer creates a tone of calm and peacefulness.

B. The writer creates a tone of excitement.

C. The writer creates a tone of self-pity.

D. The writer creates a tone of astonishment and surprise.

E. The writer creates a tone of anger and frustration.

F. The writer creates a tone of fear and menace.

G. The writer creates a tone of disappointment.

H. The writer creates a tone of solemnity and sadness.

ⓐ Which of these statements do you agree with? Tick ✓ them.

ⓑ For **each** of the statements you ticked above, identify **one** part of the text on page 18 where the writer achieves that tone. Mark and label 🖉 the relevant part of the text to identify it; for example, you could write 'calm' or 'self-pity', etc.

ⓒ Now look closely at the parts of the text you have marked and labelled. Circle Ⓐ **two or more** words or phrases in that part of the text that contribute to the tone you have identified.

ⓓ Write 🖉 two or three sentences about the tone of **one** part of the text. Aim to comment on:

• how the writer's language choices contribute to the tone you have identified

• the impact of that tone on the reader.

Commenting on words, phrases and language features

To comment on words, phrases and language features as fully and effectively as possible, you need to consider:

- how and why the writer creates patterns of language
- the impact of specific vocabulary choices within those patterns
- the range of meanings, interpretations and responses the writer may have intended
- how the writer's language choices contribute to the tone of their writing.

Look at this exam-style question:

Exam-style question

You now need to refer **only** to **source A** (lines 10 to the end).

How does the writer use language to describe her thoughts and feelings?

(12 marks)

(1) Look at this paragraph from one student's response to the question.

Identifies a pattern of language use

At the start of this part of the source, the writer focuses on her sense of smell and touch: the "fragrance of the honeysuckle" and the "cool stream". The positive connotations of "fragrance" and "cool" suggest pleasure within the limitations of her blindness and deafness. However, these limitations are soon forgotten as she effectively conveys her thoughts and feelings when she understands the purpose and the power of language. The writer contrasts the vagueness of her "misty consciousness" and the "mystery of language" with the excited, joyous tone of the "thrill" she feels when language is "revealed" to her. The writer's language choices could simply suggest her joy; however, they could also strongly suggest the sense of unconsciousness and imprisonment she felt before she was "awakened" and "set free", creating a mixture of possible responses in the reader from sympathy to elation.

Focuses on the impact of the writer's language choices on the reader

Comments on tone

Explores a range of meanings and/ or responses

Can you identify the different features of this student's response? Underline (A) or highlight (✏) the relevant parts of the paragraph then link (✏) the annotations to them.

Your turn!

You are now going to write your own answer in response to the exam-style question.

Exam-style question

You now need to refer **only** to **source A** (lines 10 to the end).

How does the writer use language to describe her thoughts and feelings?

(12 marks)

In your answer, remember to consider the writer's use of words, phrases and language features.

(1) Use the space below to gather, organise and note down ✐ your ideas.

Patterns of language choice
You could think about patterns in the writer's language choices when she describes:
- her understanding of language and meaning   • her response to this discovery.

Tone
You could think about:
- how the tone of the writer's voice changes or develops
- the tone created at specific points in the text.

A range of responses
You could think about different responses to:
- the writer   • the events described.

(2) Now write ✐ your response to the exam-style question above on paper.

Review your skills

Check up

Review your response to the exam-style question on page 23. Tick ✓ the column to show how well you think you have done each of the following.

	Not quite ✓	Nearly there ✓	Got it! ✓
identified and explored patterns of vocabulary choice	☐	☐	☐
explored layers of meaning and a variety of responses to the writer's vocabulary choices	☐	☐	☐
identified and commented on tone	☐	☐	☐

Look over all of your work in this unit. Note ✏ down the three most important things to remember when commenting on words, phrases and language features.

1. ....

2. ....

3. ....

Need more practice?

Here is another exam-style question, this time relating to source 2 on page 74: an extract from *Picturesque Sketches of London Past and Present* by Thomas Miller. You'll find some suggested points to refer to in the Answers section.

Exam-style question

You now need to refer **only** to **source 2** (line 13 to the end).

How does the writer use language to describe the fog and its effect on life in London?

(12 marks)

How confident do you feel about each of these **skills**? Colour ✏ in the bars.

① How do I focus my comments on words, phrases and language features?

② How do I develop my comments on words, phrases and language features?

③ How do I comment on tone?

Explain, comment on and analyse how writers use language and structure to achieve effects and influence readers (AO2)

④ Commenting on sentence forms

This unit will help you comment on sentence forms. The skills you will build are to:

- understand the impact that sentence forms can have
- comment in detail on the writer's use of sentence forms
- develop and build your analysis of the writer's choice of words, phrases, language features and sentence forms.

In the exam you will face questions like the one below. This is about the text on page 26. At the end of the unit you will write your own response to this question, focusing on the writer's use of sentence forms. Unit 3 focuses on how to analyse the writer's use of words, phrases and language features.

Exam-style question

You now need to refer **only** to **source A** (line 14 to the end).

How does the writer use language to influence the reader's opinion of social media?

(12 marks)

The three key questions in the **skills boosts** will help you comment on sentence forms.

① How do I identify the impact that sentence forms can have?

② How do I comment on the writer's use of sentence forms?

③ How do I comment on sentence forms and other language choices?

Read the newspaper article on page 26, written by Janet Street-Porter and published in *The Independent* in 2016. You will tackle a 21st-century non-fiction extract in the Reading section of your Paper 2 exam.

As you read, remember the following: ✓

Remember the focus of the exam question you are preparing to respond to.

Think about how the writer has tried to influence the reader's opinion of social media.

Think about how the writer has used sentence forms to add impact to those ideas.

This newspaper article appeared in *The Independent* in April 2016.

Source A Social media is making us depressed: let's learn to turn it off, Janet Street-Porter

Do Facebook and Twitter make us happier? The answer it would seem is: no. A recent survey found as many as one in five people say they feel depressed as a result of using social media. That might come as a surprise to the generation under 30; social media is part of their DNA and teenagers are rapidly losing the ability to communicate if not through their smartphones. But the stress of constantly monitoring our statuses and endlessly documenting

5 every aspect of our lives via networks like Facebook, Snapchat and Instagram is taking its toll.

Employers claim many school leavers are unprepared for the world of work, where they will have to interact with people outside their peer group and actually speak face-to-face with total strangers.

Meanwhile, there have been countless academic studies since 2015 on the negative impacts of social media, showing that its regular use leads to feelings of anxiety, isolation and low self-esteem, not to mention poor

10 sleep. We use these outlets to present a false picture of our lives to the online community; with flattering selfies and **faux**-glamorous images of holidays, parties and meals. It's as if we're starring in a movie of the life we'd like to lead, not the humdrum one we actually inhabit. An underwhelming number of shares or 'likes' can lead to debilitating feelings of inadequacy.

We post intimate fragments of our lives to total strangers, falsely believing that a 'friend' online is a real friend

15 whose opinions matter. As for Twitter, it is a vehicle for screaming, nothing more and nothing less. Best not to read tweets if you are of a vulnerable disposition.

Recently, I dared to write that cycling was being prioritised over walking in London. Cyclists, like Scottish Nationalists, are the thugs of the new era. Immediately, my words were distorted, and amplified via Twitter. I was accused of hate crimes against cycling even though I carefully said that I actually enjoyed it. I received 1,000 vile

20 and abusive messages – and they're still coming.

Twitter has an effect on one's disposition; augmenting anger and upset. Many of the women I know have come off Twitter because of the constant abuse that waits every time they pick up their phone or log in to their computer.

The latest fashion among hipsters is to have a 'digital-free' home. That could be a good move. Arianna Huffington has just written a book (*The Sleep Revolution*) citing experts who say there should be no screens in the bedroom

25 and we shouldn't use social media in the hour before lights-out.

How many times have we read a message on our phones and then spent hours in turmoil? Social media never switches off: someone, somewhere, is posting pictures, comments or messages, asking you to join a chat or wade in with an opinion. No wonder many teenagers suffer from what **shrinks** call "decision paralysis". The options are simply too enormous for any human brain to deal with.

30 For many people (not just teenagers), it seems the only way we can validate ourselves is through a screen, a habit which is just as bad for our health as over-indulging in drink or drugs. And just as addictive.

faux: fake, artificial, imitation
shrinks: psychiatrists (doctors that diagnose and treat mental illness)

1 How do I identify the impact that sentence forms can have?

The writer's choices of sentence forms can add significant impact to their ideas.

1 Which of the following features (a–f) can you identify in the sentences (A–H) taken from the newspaper article on page 26? Link ✐ each of the features.

a Questions or exclamations; for example, to encourage the reader to engage with the writer's ideas and/or add emphasis

b Punctuation for effect; for example, to create a dramatic pause and/or add emphasis to an idea

c A long sentence listing items, events or ideas to emphasise their range and impact

d A short sentence to add drama or emphasis to an idea or description

e A balanced sentence of two contrasting clauses

f A sentence in which a key idea or event is delayed until the end of the sentence, to create tension or emphasis

A Do Facebook and Twitter make us happier? ☐

B The answer it would seem is: no. ☐

C But the stress of constantly monitoring our statuses and endlessly documenting every aspect of our lives via networks like Facebook, Snapchat and Instagram is taking its toll. ☐

D It's as if we're starring in a movie of the life we'd like to lead, not the humdrum one we actually inhabit. ☐

E I received 1,000 vile and abusive messages – and they're still coming. ☐

F How many times have we read a message on our phones and then spent hours in turmoil? ☐

G Meanwhile, there have been countless academic studies since 2015 on the negative impacts of social media, showing that its regular use leads to feelings of anxiety, isolation and low self-esteem, not to mention poor sleep. ☐

H And just as addictive. ☐

2 a Read and then choose **two** of the sentences where you feel their structure adds most to the impact of the writer's ideas. Tick ✓ them.

b Write ✐ a sentence or two about each of your choices, explaining why you chose them.

....

....

....

....

....

....

....

....

2 How do I comment on the writer's use of sentence forms?

To comment effectively on sentence forms, you need to include at least two, and ideally all three, of these key features:

- writer's choice of sentence structure
- intended effect of that structural choice
- impact of that structural choice on the reader.

(1) Read one student's comment (A–H) on the first two sentences from the article on page 26.

> Do Facebook and Twitter make us happier? The answer it would seem is: no.

A. [ ] This rhetorical question engages the reader from the very beginning of the article

B. [ ] by encouraging the reader to consider their thoughts and feelings about social media.

C. [ ] The writer immediately answers her own question with an emphatic short sentence

D. [ ] using a colon to create a dramatic pause.

E. [ ] which adds further emphasis to the final word in the sentence: 'no'.

F. [ ] This opening question and answer makes clear the writer's argument,

G. [ ] which she then develops and justifies in the rest of the article,

H. [ ] effectively impressing her point of view on the reader from the start.

Write ✎ 'a', 'b', or 'c' into each box to show whether you think the phrase comments on the:

(a) writer's choice of sentence structure

(b) intended effect of that structural choice

(c) impact of that structural choice on the reader.

Put a cross ⊗ if you think the comments don't achieve any of these key features.

(2) Now write ✎ two or three sentences to comment on the final sentence of the article:

> And just as addictive.

Aim to comment on the writer's choices of sentence form, and the effect and impact of this on the reader.

....

....

....

....

....

....

③ How do I comment on sentence forms and other language choices?

Effective comments often focus on the writer's intention: the impact the writer intends his texts to have on the reader. You can link and develop your comments on the writer's choice of sentence forms, words, phrases and other language features, by exploring how they work together to achieve the writer's intention.

① Look at the writer's choices in this sentence from the extract on page 26.

> I received 1,000 vile and abusive messages – and they're still coming

a What is the writer's intention in this sentence? Annotate ✎ the quotation above with your ideas.

b How does the writer's choice of sentence forms help her to achieve her intention? Annotate ✎ the quotation above with your ideas.

c How do the writer's vocabulary choices help her to achieve her intention? Annotate ✎ the quotation above with your ideas.

d Write ✎ just **one** sentence to comment on how the writer's choices of both sentence forms and vocabulary help her to achieve her intention.

....

....

....

② Now look at the writer's choices in this sentence from the source on page 26.

> How many times have we read a message on our phones and then spent hours in turmoil?

Write ✎ one or two sentences to explore how the writer's choices in this sentence work together to help her achieve her intention.

....

....

....

....

Commenting on sentence forms

To comment effectively on sentence forms, you need to:

- identify significant sentence forms
- comment on their effect
- comment on their impact on the reader.

Now look at this exam-style question you saw at the start of the unit.

Exam-style question

You now need to refer **only** to **source A** (line 14 to the end).

How does the writer use language to influence the reader's opinion of social media?

(12 marks)

(**1**) Look at this paragraph from one student's response to the question.

| Identifies significant sentence forms |

In the middle of the article, the writer moves from general comments on social media to her own experience, highlighting the impact it has had on her personally. Using shorter sentences to add dramatic emphasis to her negative experience, she concludes the paragraph with a final, short blunt sentence detailing the quantity of "vile and abusive messages" she has received. The shocking nature of this incident is heightened still further with punctuation to create a dramatic pause before revealing that these messages are "still coming". The structure of this final sentence is entirely aimed at disturbing the reader and encouraging them to recognise the negative impact that social media can have.

| Comments on their impact on the reader |

| Comments on their effect |

Can you identify the different features of this student's response? Underline (A) the relevant parts of the paragraph then link (✎) the annotations to them.

Your turn!

You are now going to write ✐ your own answer in response to the exam-style question.

Exam-style question

You now need to refer **only** to **source A** (line 14 to the end).

How does the writer use language to influence the reader's opinion of social media?

(12 marks)

(1) Look again at the newspaper article on page 26.

    (a) Note down ✐ two or three key sentence structures the writer has used in the article. You could focus on sentence types, sentence length, punctuation or how ideas are ordered within the sentence.

    (b) Add some notes ✐ on the effect and impact on the reader of the writer's choices.

Key sentence structures	Effect and impact on the reader

(2) Now write ✐ your response to the exam-style question above on paper.

Review your skills

Check up

Review your response to the exam-style question on page 31. Tick ✓ the column to show how well you think you have done each of the following.

	Not quite ✓	Nearly there ✓	Got it! ✓
identified sentence forms crafted for effect	☐	☐	☐
commented on the impact of sentence forms	☐	☐	☐
commented on the impact of sentence forms and language choices	☐	☐	☐

Look over all of your work in this unit. Note down ✎ the three most important things to remember when commenting on sentence forms.

1. ....

2. ....

3. ....

Need more practice?

Here is another exam-style question, this time relating to source 3 on page 75: an extract from *English Journey* by J.B. Priestley. You'll find some suggested points to refer to in the Answers section.

Exam-style question

You now need to refer **only** to **source 3** (line 18 to the end).

How does the writer use language to create a powerful impression of Jarrow and Hebburn?

(12 marks)

How confident do you feel about each of these **skills?** Colour ✎ in the bars.

1 How do I identify the impact that sentence forms can have?

2 How do I comment on the writer's use of sentence forms?

3 How do I comment on sentence forms and other language choices?

Get started

Explain, comment on and analyse how writers use language and structure to achieve effects and influence readers (AO2)

⑤ Commenting on structure

This unit will help you comment on structure. The skills you will build are to:

- identify key features of whole text structure in a text
- analyse the impact of features of whole text structure
- comment effectively on the impact of whole text structure.

In the exam you will face questions like the one below. This is about the text on page 34. At the end of the unit you will write your own response to this question.

Exam-style question

You now need to think about the **whole** of **source A**.

This text is from the opening of a novel.

How has the writer structured the text to interest you as a reader?

You could write about:

- what the writer focuses your attention on at the beginning
- how and why the writer changes this focus as the source develops
- any other structural features that interest you.

(8 marks)

The three key questions in the **skills boosts** will help you comment on structure.

① How do I identify features of whole text structure?

② How do I explore the impact of whole text structure?

③ How do I develop my comments on whole text structure?

Read the source on page 34 from *The Trouble with Goats and Sheep* by Joanna Cannon, published in 2016. You will tackle a 20th- or 21st-century fiction extract in the Reading section of your Paper 1 exam.

As you read, remember the following: ✓

Remember the focus of the exam question you are preparing to respond to.

☐

Think about how the writer has selected ideas and structured the text to engage and interest readers.

☐

Underline Ⓐ or highlight ✏ any features of structure that interest you.

☐

This extract is from the opening of a novel.

Source A The Trouble with Goats and Sheep, Joanna Cannon

Number Four, The Avenue
21 June 1976

Mrs Creasy disappeared on a Monday.

I know it was a Monday, because it was the day the dustbin men came, and the avenue was filled with a smell of
5   scraped plates.

'What's he up to?' My father nodded at the lace in the kitchen window. Mr Creasy was wandering the pavement
in his shirtsleeves. Every few minutes, he stopped wandering and stood quite still, peering around his **Hillman
Hunter** and leaning into the air as though he were listening.

'He's lost his wife.' I took another slice of toast, because everyone was distracted. 'Although she's probably just
10   finally buggered off.'

'Grace Elizabeth!' My mother turned from the stove so quickly, flecks of porridge turned with her and escaped on
to the floor.

'I'm only quoting Mr Forbes,' I said, 'Margaret Creasy never came home last night. Perhaps she's finally buggered off.'

We all watched Mr Creasy. He stared into people's gardens, as though Mrs Creasy might be camping out in
15   someone else's herbaceous border.

My father lost interest and spoke into his newspaper. 'Do you listen in on all our neighbours?' he said.

'Mr Forbes was in his garden, talking to his wife. My window was open. It was accidental listening, which is allowed.'
I spoke to my father, but addressed **Harold Wilson** and his pipe, who stared back at me from the front page.

'He won't find a woman wandering up and down the avenue,' my father said, 'although he might have more luck if
20   he tried at number twelve.'

I watched my mother's face argue with a smile. They assumed I didn't understand the conversation, and it was
much easier to let them think it. My mother said I was at an *awkward age*. I didn't feel especially awkward, so I
presumed she meant that it was awkward for them.

'Perhaps she's been abducted,' I said. 'Perhaps it's not safe for me to go to school today.'

25   'It's perfectly safe,' my mother said, 'nothing will happen to you. I won't allow it.'

'How can someone just disappear?' I watched Mr Creasy, who was marching up and down the pavement. He had
heavy shoulders and stared at his shoes as he walked.

'Sometimes people need their own space,' my mother spoke to the stove, 'they get confused.'

'Margaret Creasy was confused all right.' My father turned to the sports section and snapped at the pages until
30   they were straight. 'She asked far too many questions. You couldn't get away for her rabbiting on.'

'She was just interested in people, Derek. You can feel lonely, even if you're married. And they had no children.' My
mother looked over at me as though she were considering whether the last bit made any difference at all, and
then she spooned porridge into a large bowl that had purple hearts all around the rim.

'Why are you talking about Mrs Creasy in the past tense?' I said. 'Is she dead?'

35   'No, of course not.' My mother put the bowl on the floor. 'Remington,' she shouted, 'Mummy's made your breakfast.'

Remington padded into the kitchen. He used to be a Labrador, but he'd become so fat, it was difficult to tell.

'She'll turn up,' said my father.

He'd said the same thing about next door's cat. It disappeared years ago, and no one has seen it since.

Hillman Hunter: a car
Harold Wilson: the prime minister in 1976

How do I identify features of whole text structure?

To comment effectively on the structure of a text, you need to think about the different elements the writer has selected and how they are sequenced.

① Look at some of the different elements that you might expect to find in the opening of a novel, such as the extract on page 34.

A. ☐ Interesting characters introduced and described

B. ☐ Interesting relationships between the characters implied or described

C. ☐ Key setting described

D. ☐ A strange or mysterious situation

E. ☐ A dramatic or action-packed incident

F. ☐ Humour

G. ☐ Dialogue that reveals something about the characters and their lives

H. ☐ Withholding important information to make the reader ask questions

I. ☐ Strong hints that drama or danger may be about to develop

ⓐ Tick ✓ any of the elements above that you can identify in the text.

ⓑ Now label ✎ the source on page 34 to identify where each element you have ticked is used.

② What does the writer focus on at the very beginning of the extract? How has it been designed to interest the reader? Write ✎ a sentence or two to explain your ideas.

....

....

....

....

③ How does the writer's focus change in the middle of the extract? How has it been designed to interest the reader? Write ✎ a sentence or two to explain your ideas.

....

....

....

....

④ What does the writer focus on at the very end of the extract? How has it been designed to interest the reader? Write ✎ a sentence or two explaining your ideas.

....

....

....

....

2 How do I explore the impact of whole text structure?

The selection of ideas and the way in which they are structured in a text can have a significant impact on the reader.

1 Read source A on page 34 again. As you read, consider what you learn from the extract about:

☐ each of the characters

☐ their relationship with each other

☐ what has happened in the past

☐ what is happening now

☐ what might happen in the future.

Tick ✓ the **three** elements of the text that are most interesting to you as a reader. Write ✏ a sentence or two about each one, explaining what you have learned about that character, relationship or event.

a ....
....
....

b ....
....
....

c ....
....
....

2 Now go through the extract on page 34 labelling ✏ a, b, c where the writer focuses on the characters, relationships or events you chose in question 1.

3 Look closely at the way in which the writer has structured and sequenced the three elements you chose in the opening. Why do you think the writer has structured the text in this way? Write ✏ two or three sentences to explain your ideas.

....
....
....
....
....
....
....
....

3 **How do I develop my comments on whole text structure?**

To comment effectively on whole text structure, you should comment on at least two, and ideally all four, of these key features:

- an element of whole text structure
- the intended effect of that element
- its impact on the rest of the extract
- the impact of that structural choice on the reader.

Look at some student's comments on the first sentence of the extract on page 34.

> Mrs Creasy disappeared on a Monday.

A. ☐
> This short, blunt opening statement gains the reader's attention from the very beginning of the novel.
>
> ☐ /10

B. ☐
> By including the detail that this happened on a Monday, the writer suggests that this may be important later in the story.
>
> ☐ /10

C. ☐
> Having established this fact, the rest of the opening holds the reader's attention as we search for possible reasons for Mrs Creasy's disappearance.
>
> ☐ /10

D. ☐
> After announcing this mysterious disappearance, the writer focuses on refuse collection and Mr Creasy's eccentric behaviour, suggesting his distress and his neighbours' lack of interest as they get on with their lives.
>
> ☐ /10

E. ☐
> Within a few short sentences, the writer has created a vivid and engaging impression of a dull suburban neighbourhood, a failed marriage, a scandal and perhaps even a crime.
>
> ☐ /10

F. ☐
> This short opening sentence makes the reader want to read on.
>
> ☐ /10

① Write 🖉 'a', 'b', 'c', or 'd' into each box to show whether you think the sentence:

ⓐ identifies and comments on an element of whole text structure

ⓑ comments on the intended effect of that element

ⓒ comments on its impact on the rest of the extract

ⓓ comments on the impact of that structural choice on the reader

Some sentences may cover two or more of the comments. Cross ⊗ those that don't cover any.

② How effective are each of the comments above? Give each one a mark out of 10 🖉.

③ Which comments would you include in an analysis of the extract? Tick ✓ them.

Commenting on structure

To effectively comment on structure, you should aim to:

- identify a significant structural feature of the text
- comment on its intended effect
- comment on its impact on the rest of the text
- comment on its impact on the reader.

Look at this exam-style question.

Exam-style question

You now need to think about the **whole** of **source A**.

This text is from the opening of a novel.

How has the writer structured the text to interest you as a reader?

You could write about:

- what the writer focuses your attention on at the beginning
- how and why the writer changes this focus as the source develops
- any other structural features that interest you.

(8 marks)

(1) Look at this section of the extract on page 34, with a student's annotations added.

Perhaps she has been?!

'Perhaps she's been abducted,' I said. 'Perhaps it's not safe for me to go to school today.'

'It's perfectly safe,' my mother said, 'nothing will happen to you. I won't allow it.'

+ mother's attitude to/relationship with narrator (humour/ appealing characters)

Suggests age/character of narrator (appealing narrator – want to read on)

Add your own notes (✎) to the quotation above. Remember to think about how this section of the opening has been structured to interest the reader. Focus your thoughts on:

- the effect of the writer's structural choices
- their impact on the rest of the text
- their impact on the reader.

Your turn!

You are now going to write ✐ your own answer in response to the exam-style question.

Exam-style question

You now need to think about the **whole** of **source A**.

This text is from the opening of a novel.

How has the writer structured the text to interest you as a reader?

You could write about:

- what the writer focuses your attention on at the beginning
- how and why the writer changes this focus as the source develops
- any other structural features that interest you.

(8 marks)

You should spend around 10–15 minutes on this type of question, so should aim to write three paragraphs.

1 In the boxes below, note down ✐ three significant structural features of the extract that the writer has used to interest the reader.

> 1.
>
> 2.
>
> 3.

2 Annotate ✐ each of the structural features you have identified with ideas you could use to develop your comments. Ask yourself:

- What is the effect of this feature?
- What impact does this feature have on the rest of the extract?
- What impact might this feature have on the reader?

3 Now write ✐ your response to the exam-style question above on paper.

Review your skills

Check up

Review your response to the exam-style question on page 39. Tick ✓ the column to show how well you think you have done each of the following.

	Not quite ✓	Nearly there ✓	Got it! ✓
focused on significant structural features	☐	☐	☐
considered the impact of those features	☐	☐	☐
commented effectively on the impact of those features	☐	☐	☐

Look over all of your work in this unit. Note down ✐ the three most important things to remember when commenting on structure.

1. ....

2. ....

3. ....

Need more practice?

Here is another exam-style question, this time relating to Source A on page 73: *The Secret Life of Bees* by Sue Monk Kidd. You'll find some suggested points to refer to in the Answers section.

How confident do you feel about each of these **skills?** Colour ✐ in the bars.

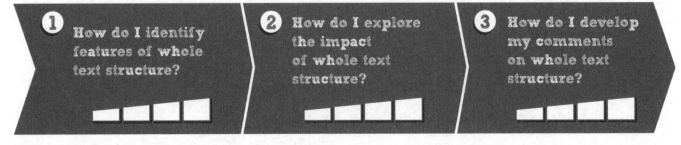

1 How do I identify features of whole text structure?

2 How do I explore the impact of whole text structure?

3 How do I develop my comments on whole text structure?

⑥ Evaluating texts

This unit will help you evaluate texts. The skills you will build are to:

- identify those features of a text that help the writer to achieve their intention
- develop analysis of a text in order to evaluate its success
- structure an effective evaluation.

In the exam you will face questions like the one below. This is about the text on page 42. At the end of the unit you will write your own response to this question.

Exam-style question

Focus this part of your answer on the second part of the source, **from line 22 to the end**.

A student, having read this section of the text, said: "This part of the text shows how different Brenda and Freda are. I can see why they react so differently to the funeral in the opening paragraphs."

To what extent do you agree?

In your response, you could:

- consider your own impressions of Brenda and Freda
- evaluate how the writer suggests their different characters
- support your opinions with quotations from the text.

(20 marks)

The three key questions in the **skills boosts** will help you evaluate texts.

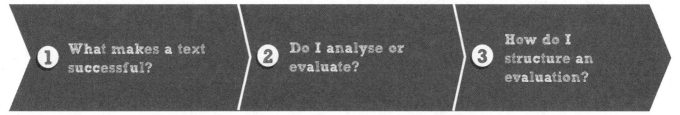

① What makes a text successful?　② Do I analyse or evaluate?　③ How do I structure an evaluation?

Read the extract on page 42. It is the opening of a novel, *The Bottle Factory Outing* by Beryl Bainbridge, first published in 1974. You will tackle a 20th- or 21st-century fiction extract in the Reading section of your Paper 1 exam.

As you read, remember the following: ⊘

Remember the focus of the exam question you are preparing to respond to.	Think about how the writer has suggested the characters of Brenda and Freda.	Think about how the writer's choices of text structure, sentence structure and vocabulary help to achieve that characterisation.
☐	☐	☐

Brenda and Freda work in a wine-bottling factory. The factory's owner, Mr Paganotti, is taking his staff on an outing.

Source A The Bottle Factory Outing, Beryl Bainbridge

The hearse stood outside the block of flats, waiting for the old lady. Freda was crying. There were some children and a dog running in and out of the line of bare black trees planted in the pavement.

'I don't know why you're crying,' said Brenda. 'You didn't know her.'

5 Four paid men in black, carrying the coffin on their shoulders, began to walk the length of the top landing. Below, on the first floor, a row of senior citizens in nighties and overcoats stood on their balconies ready to wave the old woman goodbye.

'I like it,' said Freda. 'It's so beautiful.'

Opulent at the window, she leant her beige cheek against the glass and stared out mournfully at the block of flats, moored in concrete like an ocean liner. Behind the rigging of the television aerials, the white clouds blew across

10 the sky. All hands on deck, the aged crew with lowered heads shuffled to the rails to watch the last passenger disembark.

Freda was enjoying herself. She stopped a tear with the tip of her finger and brought it to her mouth.

'I'm very moved,' she observed, as the coffin went at an acute angle down the stairs.

Brenda, who was easily embarrassed, didn't care to be seen gawping at the window. She declined to look at the

15 roof of the hearse, crowned with flowers like a Sunday hat, as the coffin was shoved into place.

'She's going,' cried Freda, and the engine started and the black car slid away from the kerb, the gladioli and the arum lilies trembling in the breeze.

'You cry easily,' said Brenda, when they were dressing to go to the factory.

'I like funerals. All those flowers – a full life coming to a close …'

20 'She didn't look as if she'd had a full life,' said Brenda. 'She only had the cat. There weren't any mourners – no sons or anything.'

'Take a lesson from it then. It could happen to you. When I go I shall have my family about me – daughters – sons – my husband, grey and distinguished, dabbing a handkerchief to his lips …'

'Men always go first,' said Brenda. 'Women live longer.'

25 'My dear, you ought to participate more. You are too cut off from life.'

When Freda spoke like that Brenda would have run into another room, had there been one. Uneasily she said, 'I do participate. More than you think.'

'You are not flotsam washed up on the shore, without recourse to the sea,' continued Freda. She was lifting one vast leg and polishing the toe of her boot on the hem of the curtains. 'When we go on the Outing you bloody well

30 better participate.'

'I can't promise,' said Brenda rebelliously.

Unlike Freda, whose idea it had been, the thought of the Outing filled her with alarm. It was bound to rain, seeing it was already October, and she could just imagine the dreary procession they would make, forlornly walking in single file across the grass, the men slipping and stumbling under the weight of the wine barrels, and Freda, face

35 distorted with fury at the weather, sinking down on to the muddy ground, unwrapping her cold chicken from its silver foil, wrenching its limbs apart under the dripping branches of the trees. Of course Freda visualised it differently. She was desperately in love with Vittorio, the trainee manager, who was the nephew of Mr Paganotti, and she thought she would have a better chance of seducing him if she could get him out into the open air, away from the bottling plant.

What makes a text successful?

To begin evaluating the success of a text, you need to have a clear overview of what the writer has set out to achieve in their text – and how their ideas support that intention.

① The question that you are going to answer gives you one student's ideas about the writer's intention.

Exam style question

A student, having read this section of the text, said:

"This part of the text shows how different Brenda and Freda are. I can see why they react so differently to the funeral in the opening paragraphs."

Tick ✓ to show whether you agree with the student's ideas.

Do you agree?   Yes, completely ☐   No, not at all ☐   I partly agree ☐

② You are now going to consider what the writer has set out to achieve in each section of the extract.

   a How would you divide the extract into two or three sections? For example, you might decide that lines 1–19 form a section that you could label 'Brenda and Freda watch the funeral'.

   Note down 🖉 your ideas below

> A.
>
> B.
>
> C.

   b How has the writer attempted to show the different characters of Brenda and Freda in each section of the extract? Add 🖉 your ideas above.

③ Now look at all of your answers to question ②. Write 🖉 one or two sentences to sum up how the writer has attempted to suggest the different characters of Brenda and Freda.

....

....

....

Do I analyse or evaluate?

In order to evaluate a text, you first need to make sure you have an overview of the text and how the writer is attempting to achieve their intention. You must then analyse **how** the writer has attempted to achieve their intention **before** you can evaluate the success of the writer's choices.

① You are going to evaluate the writer's success in suggesting the different characters of Brenda and Freda in lines 1–17 of the text on page 42. One way to tackle an evaluation is to follow these steps:

Identify and analyse the writer's intention

a Write ✎ a short sentence summing up what the writer has aimed to achieve in lines 1–17.

....

....

....

....

Identify significant choices that contribute to the writer's intention

b Choose four short quotations that demonstrate the writer's intention in lines 1–17. Underline Ⓐ them in the extract on page 42. Circle Ⓐ any significant choices of idea, text structure, sentence structure or vocabulary that make a significant contribution to the writer's intention.

Analyse the writer's choices

c Write ✎ a sentence or two commenting on how the writer's choices in lines 1–17 contribute to her intention.

....

....

....

....

Evaluate the writer's choices

d How successfully do the writer's choices in this section of the text contribute to your understanding of the differences between Brenda and Freda? Write ✎ two or three sentences to explain your ideas.

....

....

....

....

....

....

....

....

3 How do I structure an evaluation?

You can structure an evaluation by working methodically through the text, commenting on each section as you go. However, it is **much** more effective to structure an evaluation **thematically**, focusing on similar ideas or similar effects the writer has achieved or similar techniques the writer has used to achieve them.

1 One student noted these thematically related details in the text:

> *Attitudes to the funeral*
> - Freda cries but Brenda cannot understand why
>
> - Freda is moved by it; Brenda is cynical
>
> - ....
>
> - ....

What other details might you add to this list? Note 🖉 them above.

2 Look at these four details from the text:

A.
'I don't know why you're crying,' said Brenda. 'You didn't know her.'

B.
'I like it,' said Freda. 'It's so beautiful.'

C.
'I like funerals. All those flowers – a full life coming to a close …'

D.
'She didn't look as if she'd had a full life,' said Brenda. 'She only had the cat. There weren't any mourners – no sons or anything.'

a How might you connect and comment on the text above? Write 🖉 a sentence or two about each pair.

A + B: ....

....

....

C + D: ....

....

....

b Now think about how all four details work together. Write 🖉 a sentence or two to sum up the cumulative contribution that these four details make to the writer's intention to show the differences between Brenda and Freda.

....

....

....

....

....

....

Evaluating texts

A successful evaluation:

- identifies what the writer has set out to achieve
- analyses the choices the writer has made in trying to achieve their intention
- evaluates how effectively the author has achieved their intention
- is structured thematically.

Look at this exam-style question.

Exam-style question

Focus this part of your answer on the second part of the source, **from line 18 to the end**.

A student, having read this section of the text, said: "This part of the text shows how different Brenda and Freda are. I can see why they react so differently to the funeral in the opening paragraphs."

To what extent do you agree?

In your response, you could:

- consider your own impressions of Brenda and Freda
- evaluate how the writer suggests their different characters
- support your opinions with quotations from the text.

(20 marks)

(1) Then look at a paragraph from one student's response to it.

Identifies the author's intention

Analyses the writer's choices

> At the start of this section of the source, the writer contrasts Brenda's and Freda's attitudes to the funeral. While Freda seems to enjoy funerals and the thought of her own, imagining her "grey and distinguished" husband "dabbing a handkerchief to his lips", Brenda seems all too ready to destroy her romantic idealism, pointing out that "There weren't any mourners" and the deceased "only had the cat". The contrast in Freda and Brenda is emphasised in the use of sentence structure and vocabulary: Freda's dialogue is written in longer, more descriptive sentences while Brenda's is short and blunt, creating a clear picture of their two very different attitudes and the conflict between them. It is, therefore, not surprising that practical, cynical Brenda expects the Outing to be spoiled by rain while romantic Freda hopes to seduce Vittorio.

Makes a connection between related details/ ideas from the text

Evaluates the writer's success

Can you identify the different features of this student's response? Underline (A) or highlight (✏) the relevant parts of the paragraph then link (✏) the annotations to them.

Your turn!

You are now going to write your own answer in response to the exam-style question.

Exam-style question

Focus this part of your answer on the second part of the source, **from line 18 to the end.**

A student, having read this section of the text, said: "This part of the text shows how different Brenda and Freda are. I can see why they react so differently to the funeral in the opening paragraphs."

To what extent do you agree?

In your response, you could:

- consider your own impressions of Brenda and Freda
- evaluate how the writer suggests their different characters
- support your opinions with quotations from the text.

(20 marks)

Before you write your response, complete the tasks below to help you prepare.

(1) What elements of the text will you explore? Read the extract on page 42 again and, as you read, note down (✐) your ideas and any relevant quotations below.

(2) Organise and sequence your ideas in paragraphs. Sort and number (✐) them.

(3) Now write (✐) your response to the exam-style question above on paper. You should spend around 25 minutes on this question and aim to write four or five paragraphs.

Review your skills

Check up

Review your response to the exam-style question on page 47. Tick ✓ the column to show how well you think you have done each of the following.

	Not quite ✓	Nearly there ✓	Got it! ✓
identified what the writer has tried to achieve	☐	☐	☐
analysed how the writer's choices help to achieve their intention	☐	☐	☐
evaluated the writer's success	☐	☐	☐
structured my evaluation thematically	☐	☐	☐

Need more practice?

Here is another exam-style question, this time relating to source A on page 73: an extract from *The Secret Life of Bees* by Sue Monk Kidd. You'll find some suggested points to refer to in the Answers section.

Exam-style question

Focus this part of your answer on the second part of the source, from **line 18 to the end**.

A student, having read this section of the text, said: "This part of the text suggests the kind of childhood that the narrator experienced. It makes me ask lots of questions about her life."

To what extent do you agree?

In your response, you could:

* consider your own impressions of the narrator's childhood
* evaluate how the writer encourages you to ask questions
* support your opinions with quotations from the text.

(20 marks)

How confident do you feel about each of these **skills?** Colour ✐ in the bars.

① What makes a text successful?

② Do I analyse or evaluate?

③ How do I structure an evaluation?

⑦ Synthesising and comparing

This unit will help you synthesise information and ideas from two texts and compare them. The skills you will build are to:

- identify relevant explicit and implicit information in two texts
- synthesise relevant key ideas and information from two texts
- compare key ideas and information in two texts
- structure your comparison of key ideas and information from two texts.

In the exam you will face questions like the one below. This is about the texts on page 50. At the end of the unit you will write your own response to this question.

Exam-style question

You need to refer to **source A** and **source B** for this question.

Use details from **both** sources. Write a summary of the differences between the discoveries described in the two sources.

(8 marks)

The three key questions in the **skills boosts** will help you synthesise and compare similarities or differences in two texts.

① How do I synthesise key points?

② How do I compare synthesised points?

③ How do I structure my comparison?

Read the extracts on page 50, from 'Remarks on some Fossil Bones recently brought to New Orleans from Tennessee', first published in *The American Journal Of Science* in 1846, and from 'Features of Piltdown Skull "Deliberate Fakes"', an article first published in *the Manchester Guardian* newspaper in 1953. You will tackle one 19th-century non-fiction extract and one 20th- or 21st-century non-fiction extract in the Reading section of your Paper 2 exam.

As you read, remember the following:

Remember the focus of the exam question you are preparing to respond to.

Highlight any key information in Source A and Source B that is relevant to your response to the exam question.

Consider any similarities or differences in the key information you identify in each text.

In 1845, a farmer digging a well found what he believed to be a human skeleton. The size of the skeleton suggested this human would have stood around 5.5 metres (18 feet) tall.

Source A Remarks on some Fossil Bones recently brought to New Orleans from Tennessee, The American Journal Of Science

Much interest has been recently excited by the announcement of the discovery in Tennessee of the remains of a man eighteen feet high. The papers teemed with accounts of the **prodigy**, and public confidence was secured by the assertion that the distinguished physicians of the west had testified that they were human remains. About the last of December these remains reached this city; and on the first of January I was requested by a distinguished

5   surgeon here to go with him on the invitation of the proprietor to examine them, and give an opinion. At a glance it was apparent that it was nothing more than the skeleton of a young **mastodon**. Most of the vertebrae were present; the ribs mostly of wood. The pelvic arrangement was entirely of wood. The **cranium** was entirely **wanting from the lower margin of the orbits**, back; but a **raw-hide** cranium was fitted, which was much more becoming to the animal in his new capacity than the old one would have been.

10   The artificial construction was principally in the pelvis and head; and take it as thus built up, with its half human, half beast-like look, and its great hooked incisive teeth, it certainly must have conveyed to the ignorant spectator a most horrible idea of a hideous, diabolical giant, of which he no doubt dreamed for months. To one informed in such matters it really presented a most ludicrous figure.

The person who had it for exhibition was honest, I believe, in his convictions as to its being the remains of a man, having

15   been confirmed in them by numerous physicians, whose certificates he had in his possession; and having asked and received my opinion, he determined to box it up, never to be exhibited again as the remains of a human being.

prodigy: an amazing or unusual object
mastodon: a breed of dinosaur
cranium: the skull
wanting from the lower margin of the orbits: missing beneath the eye sockets
raw-hide: a kind of leather

In 1912, an amateur archaeologist claimed to have found the skull of a prehistoric ancestor of man near the village of Piltdown in Sussex. The Piltdown skull was revealed to be a fake in 1953.

Source B Features of Piltdown Skull "Deliberate Fakes", Manchester Guardian

Recent improvements in the technique of fluorine analysis made possible some of the tests which led three scientists to conclude that the **mandible** and canine tooth of the "Piltdown skull" were "deliberate fakes." The report of the three investigators – Dr. J. S. Weiner, Dr. K. P. Oakley, and Professor W. E. Le Gros Clark – appears in the Bulletin of the British Museum (Natural History).

5   Fluorine tests carried out in 1949 says the report, did not resolve the seeming contradictions between "a cranium closely similar to that of Homo Sapiens" and "a mandible and canine tooth of simian form." Not until Dr. Weiner suggested one possible explanation – "the mandible and canine tooth are actually those of a modern ape (chimpanzee or orang) which have been deliberately faked to simulate fossil specimens" – did the investigators take what they now find to be the right track.

10   Experiments produced evidence that the peculiar way in which the teeth were worn down could well have been brought about by the artificial abrasion of chimpanzee's teeth.

Other tests showed that the outer coating on the mandible and teeth did not correspond to that on the cranium. The black coating on the canine tooth turned out to be not, as the first discoverers had thought, ferruginous but "a tough, flexible paint-like substance."

15   "It is now clear (the investigators conclude) that the distinguished palaeontologists and archaeologists who took part in the excavations at Piltdown were the victims of a most elaborate and carefully prepared hoax. The faking of the mandible and canine is so extraordinarily skilful, and the perpetration of the hoax seems to have been so entirely unscrupulous and inexplicable, as to find no parallel in the history of palaeontological discovery."

mandible: jaw bone

How do I synthesise key points?

To make an effective comparison, you first need to identify key information, both **explicit** and **implicit**, from each text.

explicit: clearly stated
implicit: implied; not clearly stated

1   Look at these key pieces of information, selected from the first few lines of each text.

Source A

A.
Much interest has been recently excited by the announcement of the discovery in Tennessee of the remains of a man eighteen feet high.

C.
At a glance it was apparent that it was nothing more than the skeleton of a young mastodon.

E.
Most of the vertebrae were present; the ribs mostly of wood. The pelvic arrangement was entirely of wood… a raw-hide cranium was fitted…

Source B

B.
Recent improvements in the technique of fluorine analysis made possible some of the tests which led three scientists to conclude that the mandible and canine tooth of the "Piltdown skull" were "deliberate fakes."

D.
contradictions between "a cranium closely similar to that of Homo Sapiens" and "a mandible and canine tooth of simian form."

F.
deliberately faked to simulate fossil specimens

a   Label ✐ each one *either*:

   • **e** if the information it gives is stated **explicitly** *or*

   • **i** if the information it gives the reader is **implied**.

b   Write ✐ one or two sentences to summarise what is implied in the information that you have labelled **i**.

   ....

   ....

   ....

   ....

   ....

2   Look again at the key points of information above. Write ✐ two or three sentences summarising any similarities or differences you can identify in the two discoveries.

   ....

   ....

   ....

   ....

   ....

   ....

   ....

3   Now go through both texts on page 50 again, underlining Ⓐ or marking ✐ in the margin any further key points of information in each.

2 How do I compare synthesised points?

When you are asked to identify similarities and differences in two texts, you need to synthesise relevant information from both texts. A particularly effective comparison will synthesise a range of linked evidence from different parts of each text.

(1) Look at one student's comment on the two texts on page 50.

> *Both texts provide evidence of fraud, suggesting that neither the Piltdown skull nor the giant's skeleton was what it appeared to be.*

Identify **four** pieces of evidence, two from each text, to support this statement. Underline (A) them in the texts on page 50 and label (✐) them 1A, 1B, 1C and 1D.

(2) Now look closely at these four pieces of information from the two texts on page 50.

Source A

…it certainly must have conveyed to the ignorant spectator a most horrible idea of a hideous, diabolical giant… To one informed in such matters it really presented a most ludicrous figure.

…public confidence was secured by the assertion that the distinguished physicians of the west had testified that they were human remains.

Source B

…distinguished palaeontologists and archaeologists who took part in the excavations at Piltdown were the victims of a most elaborate and carefully prepared hoax.

The faking of the mandible and canine is so extraordinarily skilful… as to find no parallel in the history of palaeontological discovery.

a Write (✐) a sentence to explain how you could link the two pieces of information from source A.

....

....

....

b Now write (✐) a sentence to explain how you could link the two pieces of information from source B.

....

....

....

c Write (✐) a sentence or two to summarise any differences between source A and source B, using all four pieces of information as evidence.

....

....

....

③ How do I structure my comparison?

When you have identified three or four key points of comparison between the texts, you can use them to structure your response.

① Look at the exam-style question on page 49.

   a Which of these points of comparison would you use to respond to the question? Tick ✓ them.

		✓	✏
A.	Source A is written from an expert point of view; source B reports an expert point of view.	☐	☐
B.	Source A describes a "ludicrous" attempt at fraud; source B describes a very convincing fraud.	☐	☐
C.	Source B explains how the fraud was carried out; source A does not explain this.	☐	☐
D.	Source B suggests why experts were deceived by the fraud; source A does not.	☐	☐
E.	Source A creates a dramatic image of the discovery whereas source B focuses on the scale of the fraud.	☐	☐
F.	Both discoveries are frauds but the discovery described in source A was a whole skeleton while the discovery described in source B was just a skull.	☐	☐

   b In what order would you sequence your chosen points of comparison? Number ✏ them.

② Now look at these sentences taken from one paragraph of a student's response to the exam-style question above.

		✓	✏
A.	Source A describes a "ludicrous" fraud.	☐	☐
B.	Source B describes a very convincing fraud.	☐	☐
C.	Although the discovery described in source B was much larger and the fraud much bolder, it was also a more obvious fraud.	☐	☐
D.	Source A describes a skeleton made up of "the skeleton of a young mastodon", wooden ribs and pelvis and a cranium made of raw-hide.	☐	☐
E.	Source B describes a similarly mismatched discovery: "a cranium closely similar to that of Homo Sapiens" and "a mandible and canine tooth of simian form."	☐	☐
F.	According to Source A, it was clearly a fraud to "one informed in such matters".	☐	☐
G.	Source B, however, emphasises how "skilful" and "carefully prepared" the hoax was.	☐	☐

   a Which ideas would you include in your response to the exam-style question above? Tick ✓ them.

   b How would you sequence the ideas you have chosen? Number ✏ them.

Synthesising and comparing

To synthesise and compare relevant information in two texts, you need to:

- identify relevant key information, both explicit and implicit
- identify and link related information from each text
- organise your comparison effectively.

Note: you do not need to analyse and compare the writer's choices in this type of question. This skill is tested in questions that ask you to compare the writer's viewpoints, perspectives and ideas, which is the focus of Unit 8.

Look at this exam-style question.

Exam-style question

You need to refer to **source A** and **source B** for this question.

Use details from **both** sources. Write a summary of the differences between the discoveries described in the two sources.

(8 marks)

(1) Now look at a paragraph from one student's response to the exam-style question above.

> Source A describes the impression which the giant skeleton had on the media, which "teemed with accounts of the prodigy" and the impact it might have on an "ignorant spectator", emphasising how strange and terrifying its "half human, half beast-like" appearance and "great, hooked incisive teeth" would be. The writer seems to be implying that those who faked the skeleton were relying on people's ignorance and the dramatic appearance of the creature to make them some money. Source B, however, focuses on the motives of those who perpetrated the fraud of the Piltdown skull, rather than the impact it had, and seems to wonder what those motives might be. The writer explicitly describes the fraud as "unscrupulous and inexplicable", and so "skilful" that even "distinguished palaeontologists and archaeologists" were "victims" of the deception. There is, however, no suggestion as to why the fraud was perpetrated.

a Which of these key features of a paragraph of effective synthesis and comparison has this student achieved? Tick ✓ them.

   i. Links information from each text

   ii. Refers to explicit and implied information

   iii. Comments on the implications of implied information

   iv. Compares information from the two texts

b Annotate ✎ the paragraph above, to show where the student has achieved each key feature you have ticked.

Your turn!

You are now going to write your own answer in response to the exam-style question.

Exam-style question

You need to refer to **source A** and **source B** for this question.

Use details from **both** sources. Write a summary of the differences between the discoveries described in the two sources. **(8 marks)**

1. In the space below, note down 🖊 at least three different points of comparison you can use in your response.

2. For each point, note down 🖊 two pieces of evidence from each source. Aim to select evidence that supports your point and will allow you to compare the two texts.

3. For each point, note down 🖊 some ways in which you can compare the evidence and the texts.

	Source A	Source B	Similar or different? In what ways?
The writer's intention/ideas and attitudes			
Key evidence			
Key choices to explore in that evidence			

4. Now write 🖊 your response to the exam-style question above on paper.

Review your skills

Check up

Review your response to the exam-style question on page 55. Tick ✓ the column to show how well you think you have done each of the following.

	Not quite ✓	Nearly there ✓	Got it! ✓
identified and linked key information from both texts, both explicit and implied	☐	☐	☐
ordered points of comparison effectively	☐	☐	☐
made effective, relevant comparisons	☐	☐	☐

Look over all of your work in this unit. Note down ✏ the three most important things to remember when synthesising and comparing.

1. ....

2. ....

3. ....

Need more practice?

Here is another exam-style question, this time relating to source 2 on page 74, an extract from *Picturesque Sketches of London Past and Present* by Thomas Miller, and source 3 on page 75, an extract from *English Journey* by J.B. Priestley. You'll find some suggested points to refer to in the Answers section.

Exam-style question

You need to refer to **source A** and **source B** for this question.

Use details from **both** sources. Write a summary of the differences between the writers' experiences of London and Jarrow.

(8 marks)

How confident do you feel about each of these **skills?** Colour ✏ in the bars.

① How do I synthesise key points?

② How do I compare synthesised points?

③ How do I structure my comparison?

⑧ Comparing ideas and attitudes

This unit will help you compare the writers' ideas and attitudes in two texts. The skills you will build are to:

- identify key areas for comparison
- compare the writers' ideas, attitudes and intentions
- explore how the writers' ideas, attitudes and intentions are conveyed
- develop an analytical comparison of the writers' choices.

In the exam you will face questions like the one below. This is about the texts on page 58. At the end of the unit you will write your own response to this question.

Exam-style question

For this question, you need to refer to the **whole of source A**, together with the **whole of source B**.

Compare how the two writers convey their different attitudes to the animals they describe.

In your answer, you could:

- compare their different attitudes
- compare the methods they use to convey their attitudes
- support your ideas with references to both texts.

(16 marks)

The three key questions in the **skills boosts** will help you compare writers' ideas and attitudes.

① How do I identify relevant ideas and attitudes?   **② How do I compare ideas and attitudes?**   **③ How do I develop my comparison?**

Read the extracts on page 58 from 'My Struggle with a Tiger', an article published in *The Boy's Own Paper* in 1879, and *H is for Hawk* by Helen Macdonald, published in 2014. You will tackle two non-fiction extracts, one from the 19th-century and one from the 20th- or 21st-century, in the Reading section of your Paper 2 exam.

As you read, remember the following: ✓

The writer's ideas and attitudes in the two texts: how do they describe and respond to animals?	Any similarities or differences between the two writers' ideas and attitudes.	Any similarities or differences in the ways the two writers express their ideas and attitudes.
☐	☐	☐

Charles Jamrach imported and sold wild animals to zoos and circuses. In this article, he describes what happened when his men were unloading a tiger in his yard in central London.

Source A My Struggle with a Tiger, Charles Jamrach

I had given directions to my men to place a den containing a very ferocious full-grown Bengal tiger, with its iron-barred front close against the wall.

All of a sudden I heard a crash, and to my horror found the big tiger had pushed out the back part of his den with his hind-quarters, and was walking down the yard into the street, which was then full of people. As soon as he got
5   into the street, a boy of about nine years of age put out his hand to stroke the beast's back, when the tiger seized him by the shoulder and ran down the street with the lad hanging in his jaws. I dashed after the brute, and got hold of him but he was too strong for me, and dragged me, too, along with him.

My men had been seized with the same panic as the bystanders, but now I discovered one lurking round a corner, so I shouted to him to come with a crowbar; he fetched one, and hit the tiger three tremendous blows over the
10 eyes.

It was only now he released the boy. His jaws opened and his tongue protruded about seven inches. I thought the brute was dead or dying, and let go of him, but no sooner had I done so than he jumped up again. In the same moment I seized the crowbar myself, and gave him, with all the strength I had left, a blow over his head. He seemed to be quite cowed, and, turning tail, went back towards the stables, which fortunately were open. I drove
15 him into the yard, and closed the doors at once. Looking round for my tiger, I found he had sneaked into a large empty den that stood open at the bottom of the yard. Two of my men pushed down the iron-barred sliding-door of the den; and so my tiger was safe again under lock and key.

Helen Macdonald goes out one morning, hoping to catch a glimpse of a goshawk, a rare bird of prey.

Source B H is for Hawk, Helen Macdonald

It was 8.30 exactly. I was looking down at a little sprig of mahonia growing out of the turf, its oxblood leaves like buffed pigskin. I glanced up. And then I saw my goshawks. There they were. A pair, soaring above the canopy in the rapidly warming air. There was a flat, hot hand of sun on the back of my neck, but I smelt ice in my nose, seeing those goshawks soaring. I smelt ice and bracken stems and pine resin. Goshawk cocktail. They were on the
5   soar. Goshawks in the air are a complicated grey colour. Not slate grey, nor pigeon grey. But a kind of raincloud grey, and despite their distance, I could see the big powder-puff of white undertail feathers, fanned out, with the thick, blunt tail behind it, and that superb bend and curve of the secondaries of a soaring goshawk that makes them utterly unlike sparrowhawks. These goshawks weren't fully displaying: there was none of the skydiving I'd read about in books. But they were loving the space between each other, and carving it into all sorts of beautiful
10 concentric chords and distances. A couple of flaps, and the male, the tiercel, would be above the female, and then he'd drift north of her, and then slip down, fast, like a knife-cut, a smooth calligraphic scrawl underneath her, and she'd dip a wing, and then they'd soar up again. They were above a stand of pines, right there. And then they were gone. One minute my pair of goshawks was describing lines from physics textbooks in the sky, and then nothing at all. I don't remember looking down, or away. Perhaps I blinked. Perhaps it was as simple as that. And in that tiny
15 black gap which the brain disguises they'd dived into the wood.

1 How do I identify relevant ideas and attitudes?

Before you can compare two writers' ideas and attitudes, you need to:
- identify each writer's intention – the impact they intend the text to have on the reader
- look very closely at each text, to identify the most significant and/or interesting ideas and attitudes that help the writer to achieve their intention.

1 Look again at the two texts on page 58.

   a Write 🖉 **one** sentence summing up each writer's intention.

   Source A: ....

   ....

   Source B: ....

   ....

   b Now write 🖉 **one** sentence comparing the two writers' intentions. Think about:

   - how are they similar
   - how are they different?

   ....

   ....

   ....

2 a Circle Ⓐ **three** key quotes in each of the texts on page 58 that reveal the most interesting or significant ideas and attitudes in each text.

   b Look at the quotations you have selected. Note down 🖉 at least three words or phrases to describe each writer's ideas and attitudes about animals.

Source A	Source B
1	1 ....
....	....
....	....
2	2 ....
....	....
....	....
3	3 ....
....	....
....	....

   c Circle Ⓐ and draw 🖉 a line linking any **similar** ideas or attitudes in the two texts.

   d Underline Ⓐ and draw 🖉 a line linking any very **different** ideas or attitudes in the two texts.

② How do I compare ideas and attitudes?

To write a perceptive comparison of two writers' ideas and attitudes, you need to look closely at **every** choice the writers have made.

① You can often find the most significant and interesting ideas and attitudes by reading between the lines.

a Look at some of the evidence that one student identified in these two texts. What does each piece of evidence reveal about the writers' ideas and attitudes about the animals they are describing? Annotate 🖉 each piece of evidence with your ideas.

Source A

A.
> I seized the crowbar myself, and gave him, with all the strength I had left, a blow over his head.

B.
> my tiger was safe again under lock and key

Source B

C.
> I saw my goshawks

D.
> I smelt ice in my nose, seeing those goshawks soaring.

b Write 🖉 a sentence or two comparing what these four quotations reveal about the writers and their relationships with animals.

....

....

....

....

② One way to compare texts is to think about the selection and structure of ideas the writer has used. Look at this summary of each text.

Source A

- A wild animal dealer unloads a tiger in a cage.
- The tiger escapes; the dealer hits him with a crowbar.
- Luckily the tiger sneaks into an empty den and is trapped again.

Source B

- The writer goes out one morning and spots a pair of goshawks by chance.
- She describes their flight.
- The goshawks suddenly disappear.

The middle section of each text seems to reveal the most about the writers' ideas and attitudes about animals. However, you need to think about the whole extract.

How do the opening and ending sections of each text add to your understanding of the writers' ideas and attitudes? Write 🖉 a sentence or two about each source on page 58.

Source A: ....

....

Source B: ....

....

③ How do I develop my comparison?

The most effective comparisons **analyse and compare** the writers' choices and how they contribute to the writer's intention: the impact the writer intends their text to have on the reader.

① What is the writer's intention in source A and in source B on page 58? Summarise ✐ each writer's intention in two or three words.

The writer of source A's intention: ....

The writer of source B's intention: ....

② Think about how the writer's vocabulary choices in these quotations might contribute to their intention.

Source A

> a boy of about nine years of age put out his hand to stroke the beast's back, when the tiger seized him

Source B

> he'd drift north of her, and then slip down, fast, like a knife-cut, a smooth calligraphic scrawl, underneath her

How do the writers' vocabulary choices help them to achieve their intention and convey their ideas and attitudes? Write ✐ a sentence or two comparing them.

....

....

....

....

....

③ Now look at some of the sentence structures the two writers use.

The writer of **source A** uses long sentences to list a series of events:

> All of a sudden I heard a crash, and to my horror found the big tiger had pushed out the back part of his den with his hind-quarters, and was walking down the yard into the street, which was then full of people.

The writer of **source B** uses a lot of short sentences:

> And then I saw my goshawks. There they were.

> And then they were gone.

What do these sentence structure choices contribute to the tone and/or pace of each text? Write ✐ a sentence or two comparing how the two writers use shorter sentences.

....

....

....

....

....

④ Read the two texts carefully again. Underline Ⓐ and annotate ✐ any other significant vocabulary or sentence structure choices in each text on page 58, noting their contribution to the writers' intentions.

Comparing ideas and attitudes

To write an effective comparison of two texts, you need to:

- identify each writer's intention, ideas and attitudes
- read each text carefully, looking for significant evidence that explicitly or implicitly reveals each writer's intention, ideas and attitudes
- identify significant points of comparison between the two texts
- explore and compare each writer's choices and their contribution to the writer's intention, ideas and attitudes.

Look again at the exam-style question on page 57.

1 Now look at the paragraph below, written by a student in response to this exam-style question.

> These texts suggest very different attitudes to animals. The writer of source A conveys the sense of a battle between man and a dangerous, threatening animal: the tiger is "ferocious", a "brute", and the writer has no shame in hitting the "beast" with a crowbar. Once subdued, the creature is described as "my tiger", suggesting domination and ownership. The writer of source B describes a much more positive encounter with wild animals, expressing her admiration at the goshawks "soaring" through and "carving" the sky. She too uses the possessive pronoun, describing the birds as "my goshawks", but in this text it suggests, not ownership, but the strong personal bond she feels between human and animal.

a Annotate the paragraph, underlining Ⓐ and labelling to show where in the paragraph this student has:

   i. identified a significant similarity or difference in the writers' ideas and attitudes

   ii. supported their ideas with range of evidence from both texts

   iii. compared how the writers' choices convey their ideas and attitudes and achieve their intention.

b How could this student improve the paragraph above? Write a sentence or two summarising your ideas.

....

....

....

....

....

Your turn!

You are now going to write your own answer in response to the exam-style question.

Exam-style question

For this question, you need to refer to the **whole of source A**, together with the **whole of source B**.

Compare how the two writers convey their different attitudes to the animals they describe.

In your answer, you could:

- compare their different attitudes
- compare the methods they use to convey their attitudes
- support your ideas with references to both texts.

(16 marks)

1 You should spend 20–25 minutes on this kind of question, so should aim to write 🖉 four or five paragraphs. Use the space below to gather and develop your ideas.

	Source A	Source B	Similar or different? In what ways?
The writer's ideas and attitudes			
Key evidence			
Key choices to explore in that evidence			

2 Now write 🖉 your response to the exam-style question above on paper.

Review your skills

Check up

Review your response to the exam-style question on page 63. Tick ✓ the column to show how well you think you have done each of the following.

	Not quite ✓	**Nearly there** ✓	**Got it** ✓
identified key areas for comparison	☐	☐	☐
compared the writers' ideas, attitudes and intentions	☐	☐	☐
explored how the writers' ideas, attitudes and intentions are conveyed	☐	☐	☐
developed an analytical comparison of the writers' choices	☐	☐	☐

Need more practice?

Here is another exam-style question, this time relating to source 2 on page 74, an extract from *Picturesque Sketches of London Past and Present* by Thomas Miller, and source 3 on page 75, an extract from *English Journey* by J.B. Priestley. You'll find some suggested points to refer to in the Answers section.

Exam-style question

For this question, you need to refer to the **whole of source 2**, together with the **whole of source 3**.

Compare how the two writers convey their different attitudes to and experiences of the places they describe.

In your answer, you should:

- compare their different attitudes and experiences
- compare the methods they use to convey their attitudes and experiences
- support your ideas with references to both texts.

(16 marks)

How confident do you feel about each of these **skills?** Colour ✏ in the bars.

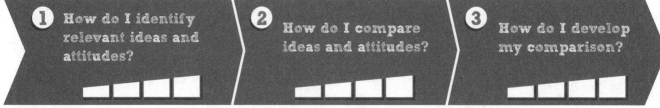

1 How do I identify relevant ideas and attitudes?

2 How do I compare ideas and attitudes?

3 How do I develop my comparison?

9 Expressing your ideas clearly and precisely

This unit will help you learn how to express your ideas clearly and precisely. The skills you will build are to:

- develop the depth and breadth of your analysis by embedding a range of evidence within it
- choose vocabulary that expresses your ideas precisely
- use a range of sentence structures to express your ideas with clarity.

In the exam you will face questions like the one below. This is about the text on page 66. At the end of the unit you will write your own response to this question.

Exam-style question

You now need to refer **only** to **source A**, a letter from the Chairman of the London Hospital to *The Times* newspaper.

How does the writer use language to make you, the reader, feel sympathy for Joseph Merrick?

(12 marks)

The three key questions in the **skills boosts** will help you express your ideas clearly and precisely.

 1 How do I express my ideas concisely?

 2 How do I express my ideas precisely?

 3 How do I express my ideas clearly?

Read the extract on page 66, from a letter originally published in *The Times* newspaper in 1886. You will tackle a 19th-century non-fiction extract in the Reading section of your Paper 2 exam.

As you read, remember the following:

Remember the focus of the exam question you are preparing to respond to

Think about where in the text the writer has tried to make the reader feel sympathy for Joseph Merrick.

Think about how the writer's choices of words and phrases, language features and sentence forms help to achieve their intention.

In 1886, the Chairman of the London Hospital wrote a letter to *The Times* newspaper, asking for the public's support in helping Joseph Merrick, known as 'The Elephant Man'. With the public donations that this letter prompted, Merrick was cared for at the London Hospital for the rest of his short life.

Source A A letter in *The Times* newspaper, 1886

Sir, – I am authorized to ask your powerful assistance in bringing to the notice of the public the following most exceptional case. There is now in a little room off one of our attic wards a man named Joseph Merrick, aged about 27, a native of Leicester, so dreadful a sight that he is unable even to come out by daylight to the garden. He has been called "the elephant man" on account of his terrible deformity. I will not shock your readers with any detailed
5   description of his infirmities, but only one arm is available for work.

Some 18 months ago, Mr Treves, one of the surgeons of the London Hospital, saw him as he was exhibited in a room off the Whitechapel-road. The poor fellow was then covered by an old curtain, endeavouring to warm himself over a brick which was heated by a lamp. As soon as a sufficient number of pennies had been collected by the manager at the door, poor Merrick threw off his curtain and exhibited himself in all his deformity. He and the
10   manager went halves in the net proceeds of the exhibition, until at last the police stopped the exhibition of his deformities as against public decency.

The police rightly prevent his being personally exhibited again; he cannot go out into the streets, as he is everywhere so mobbed that existence is impossible; he cannot, in justice to others, be put in the general ward of a workhouse, and from such, even if possible, he shrinks with the greatest horror; he ought not to be detained in
15   our hospital (where he is occupying a private ward, and being treated with the greatest kindness – he says he has never before known in his life what quiet and rest were), since his case is incurable and not suited, therefore, to our overcrowded general hospital; the incurable hospitals refuse to take him in even if we paid for him in full, and the difficult question therefore remains what is to be done for him.

Terrible though his appearance is, so terrible indeed that women and nervous persons fly in terror from the
20   sight of him, and that he is debarred from seeking to earn his livelihood in an ordinary way, yet he is superior in intelligence, can read and write, is quiet, gentle, not to say even refined in his mind. Through all the miserable vicissitudes of his life he has carried about a painting of his mother to show that she was a decent and presentable person, and as a memorial of the only one who was kind to him in life until he came under the kind care of the nursing staff of the London Hospital and the surgeon who has befriended him.

25   It is a case of singular affliction brought about through no fault of himself; he can but hope for quiet and privacy during a life which Mr Treves assures me is not likely to be long.

Can any of your readers suggest to me some fitting place where he can be received? And then I feel sure that, when that is found, charitable people will come forward and enable me to provide him with such accommodation.

I have the honour to be, Sir, yours obediently,
30   F. C. Carr-Gomm,
Chairman London Hospital.

How do I express my ideas concisely?

Embedding a range of evidence within your comments demonstrates that you can identify significant choices the writer has made. It also allows you to focus your analysis closely on them.

(1) Compare these two comments on the text on page 66.

Student A

> The writer highlights the treatment that Merrick suffered before he came to the London Hospital, describing how he was "endeavouring to warm himself over a brick which was heated by a lamp. As soon as a sufficient number of pennies had been collected by the manager at the door, poor Merrick threw off his curtain and exhibited himself in all his deformity." The image of him "trying to warm himself" suggests how hard his life was and how badly he was treated. The word "exhibited" makes him sound like an object not a person.

Student B

> The writer clearly describes the life from which Merrick was rescued. The image of him warming himself "over a brick... heated by a lamp" as his manager collected "pennies" suggests poverty and degradation which, combined with the humiliation of being "covered by an old curtain" and then being "exhibited... in all his deformity", suggests that Merrick had to survive by being treated like an object.

Which is the most effective, and most effectively expressed, comment? Why?
Write ✏ a sentence or two to explain your choice.

....

....

....

....

(2) Now look at this comment on source A on page 66.

> The writer adds to the reader's sympathy by explaining that "he is occupying a private ward, and being treated with the greatest kindness – he says he has never before known in his life what quiet and rest were". This creates sympathy because it suggests that Merrick has never been treated kindly before and has always lived a difficult life.

Rewrite ✏ the comment above, aiming to embed key elements of the quotation and sharpen the focus of the analysis.

....

....

....

....

② How do I express my ideas precisely?

Sometimes, ideas are best and most clearly expressed using fewer, more carefully chosen words.

① Look at one student's notes on the impression the writer creates of Joseph Merrick in the extract on page 66.

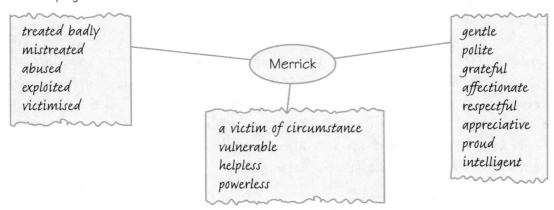

treated badly
mistreated
abused
exploited
victimised

Merrick

gentle
polite
grateful
affectionate
respectful
appreciative
proud
intelligent

a victim of circumstance
vulnerable
helpless
powerless

a Decide which of the noted words and phrases accurately and appropriately describes how the writer presents the character of Joseph Merrick. Cross out ⊗ any words and phrases that are **not** accurate or appropriate.

b Complete ✏ the sentence below by choosing the **three** most precise words or phrases to describe how the writer presents the character of Joseph.

The writer creates the impression that Merrick is ....

....

....

....

② Compare these two comments on source A on page 66.

Student A

> The writer does not give any details of how Merrick is deformed, but he does give examples of ways in which people have reacted when they have seen him.

Student B

> The writer withholds details of Merrick's condition, focusing instead on people's reactions to it.

How has Student B expressed the same ideas in far fewer words? Annotate ✏ the responses to explain your ideas.

③ Write ✏ **one** sentence commenting on the impression the writer creates of Mr Treves and the staff at the London Hospital. Aim to express your ideas as precisely and as concisely as possible.

....

....

....

....

3 How do I express my ideas clearly?

You can use longer, multiclause sentences to link and develop complex ideas. You can also use shorter sentences to summarise, emphasise or clarify your ideas.

1 **a** Compare these two comments on the extract on page 66. Circle Ⓐ any differences you can spot.

Student A

> The writer withholds details of Merrick's condition, focusing instead on the response it creates, describing how he is "so dreadful a sight" that he cannot go outside "by daylight", implying that he cannot be seen or, we are later told, he will be "mobbed", making his "existence… impossible", suggesting he is existing rather than living, and even that existence has been destroyed by his condition.

Student B

> The writer withholds details of Merrick's condition, focusing instead on the response it creates. Merrick is "so dreadful a sight" that he cannot go outside "by daylight", implying that he cannot be seen or, we are later told, he will be "mobbed", making his "existence… impossible". He is existing rather than living, and even that existence has been destroyed by his condition.

b Which version is the most clearly expressed? Write ✏ a sentence or two to explain your choice.

....

....

....

2 **a** Experiment with restructuring ✏ all the ideas and comments in this very long sentence in two or three shorter sentences.

> The writer goes to some lengths to create an impression of Merrick as an intelligent and affectionate man, listing his appreciation of the "quiet and rest" of the hospital, his ability to "read and write" and the fact that he is "quiet" and "gentle", but the portrait of his mother that he carries because she was "the only one who was kind to him" is perhaps the most revealing and sympathetic detail of all.

....

....

....

b Which version is the most clearly expressed: yours or the original version? Write ✏ a sentence or two to explain your choice.

....

....

....

Expressing your ideas clearly and precisely

To express your ideas clearly and precisely, you need to:

- use short embedded quotations, to sharpen your analysis and express it concisely
- choose vocabulary that expresses your ideas precisely
- choose sentence structures that express your ideas clearly.

Now look at the exam-style question you saw at the start of the unit.

> **Exam-style question**
>
> You now need to refer **only** to **source A**, a letter from the Chairman of the London Hospital to *The Times* newspaper.
>
> How does the writer use language to make you, the reader, feel sympathy for Joseph Merrick?
>
> (12 marks)

(**1**) Look at a short paragraph from one student's response to this question.

> The writer makes one final plea for Merrick at the end of his letter. He refers to Merrick's "singular affliction", emphasising Merrick's "exceptional" suffering, points out that his life "is not likely to be long", and suggests that even a short experience of "quiet and privacy" is all that he can "hope for". The picture created is of a terminally ill man, suffering terribly, whose short life would be greatly improved with the protection of the public's kindness.

Write ✎ two or three sentences to state what this student has done well and what they could do to improve. Think about:

- their use of embedded evidence
- their choice of vocabulary
- how they have used longer sentences to link ideas
- how they have used shorter sentences for summary, clarity or emphasis.

....

....

....

....

....

....

....

Your turn!

You are now going to write just **one** paragraph in response to this exam-style question.

Exam-style question

You now need to refer **only** to **source** A, a letter from the Chairman of the London Hospital to *The Times* newspaper.

How does the writer use language to make you, the reader, feel sympathy for Joseph Merrick?

(12 marks)

(1) Choose one section of the extract that you will focus on in your paragraph. Write 🖉 it in the space below.

(2) Underline Ⓐ or circle Ⓐ the writer's choices that you will focus on in your paragraph.

(3) Annotate 🖉 the choices you have circled or underlined, noting the comments you could include in your paragraph.

(4) Write 🖉 your paragraph in the space below.

(5) Review your writing, asking yourself:

- Can I shorten any longer quotations and embed them more effectively to sharpen my analysis?
- Can I improve any of my vocabulary choices to express my ideas more precisely?
- Can I link any of my ideas more clearly in longer sentences?
- Can I shorten any sentences to summarise, clarify or add emphasis to any of my ideas?

Make any necessary changes 🖉 to your paragraph, so that it is as clearly and precisely expressed as possible.

Review your skills

Check up

Review your response to the exam-style question on page 71. Tick ✓ the column to show how well you think you have done each of the following.

	Not quite ✓	Nearly there ✓	Got it! ✓
used embedded quotations to sharpen analysis	☐	☐	☐
selected precise vocabulary	☐	☐	☐
selected sentence structures for clarity	☐	☐	☐

Look over all of your work in this unit. Note down ✐ the three most important things to remember when reviewing the clarity and precision of your analytical writing.

1. ....

2. ....

3. ....

Need more practice?

You can EITHER:

① Look again at your paragraph written in response to the exam-style question on page 71. Rewrite it ✐, experimenting with different vocabulary choices and sentence structures, linking your ideas in different ways. Which are most effective in expressing your ideas clearly and precisely?

AND/OR

② Write ✐ a further paragraph in response to the exam-style question, focusing closely on your use of quotation, vocabulary choice and sentence structures.

How confident do you feel about each of these **skills?** Colour ✐ in the bars.

① How do I express my ideas concisely?

② How do I express my ideas precisely?

③ How do I express my ideas clearly?

More practice texts

This is the opening of a novel. It is 1964. Lily is 14. She lives in South Carolina, USA.

Source 1 The Secret Life of Bees, Sue Monk Kidd

At night I would lie in bed and watch the show, how bees squeezed through the cracks of my bedroom wall and flew circles around the room, making that propeller sound, a high-pitched zzzzzz that hummed along my skin. I watched their wings shining like bits of chrome in the dark and felt the longing build in my chest. The way those bees flew, not even looking for a flower, just flying for the feel of the wind, split my heart down its seam.

5 During the day I heard them tunneling through the walls of my bedroom, sounding like a radio tuned to static in the next room, and I imagined them in there turning the walls into honeycombs, with honey seeping out for me to taste.

The bees came the summer of 1964, the summer I turned fourteen and my life went spinning off into a whole new orbit, and I mean whole new orbit. Looking back on it now, I want to say the bees were sent to me. I want to say
10 they showed up like the angel Gabriel appearing to the Virgin Mary, setting events in motion I could never have guessed. I know it is presumptuous to compare my small life to hers, but I have reason to believe she wouldn't mind; I will get to that. Right now it's enough to say that despite everything that happened that summer, I remain tender toward the bees.

* * * * *

July 1, 1964, I lay in bed, waiting for the bees to show up, thinking of what Rosaleen had said when I told her about
15 their nightly visitations.

"Bees swarm before death," she'd said.

Rosaleen had worked for us since my mother died. My daddy – who I called T. Ray because "Daddy" never fit him – had pulled her out of the peach orchard, where she'd worked as one of his pickers. She had a big round face and a body that sloped out from her neck like a pup tent, and she was so black that night seemed to seep from her skin.
20 She lived alone in a little house tucked back in the woods, not far from us, and came every day to cook, clean, and be my stand-in mother. Rosaleen had never had a child herself, so for the last ten years I'd been her pet guinea pig.

Bees swarm before death. She was full of crazy ideas that I ignored, but I lay there thinking about his one, wondering if the bees had come with my death in mind. Honestly, I wasn't that disturbed by the idea. Every one of
25 those bees could have descended on me like a flock of angels and stung me till I died, and it wouldn't have been the worst thing to happen. People who think dying is the worst thing don't know a thing about life.

My mother died when I was four years old. It was a fact of life, but if I brought it up, people would suddenly get interested in their hangnails and cuticles, or else distant places in the sky, and seem not to hear me. Once in a while, though, some caring soul would say, "Just put it out of your head, Lily. It was an accident. You didn't mean to
30 do it."

During the 19th century, a thick smog sometimes covered London, created by particles of soot from the burning of huge amounts of coal in people's homes and in factories.

Source 2 Picturesque Sketches of London Past and Present, Thomas Miller

SUCH of our readers as have never been in London in November can scarcely imagine what it is to grope their way through a downright thorough London fog. It is something like being imbedded in a dilution of yellow **peas-pudding**, just thick enough to get through it without being wholly choked or completely suffocated. Every time you open your mouth you partake of it, and all day long you are compelled to burn lights, and, in addition
5   to the fog, inhale the fumes from gas, candle, or lamp, which have no more chance of escape than you have, so burn on dim, yellow, and sulkily, as if the very lights needed all the warmth they could obtain, and thus confine themselves to illuminating the smallest possible space.

The whole city seems covered with a crust, and all the light you can see beneath it appears as if struggling through the huge yellow basin it overspreads. You fancy that all the smoke which had ascended for years from
10   the thousands of London chimneys had fallen down all at once, after having rotted somewhere above the clouds; smelling as if it had been kept too long, and making you wheeze and sneeze as if all the colds in the world were rushing into your head for warmth, and did not care a straw about killing a few thousands of people, so long as they could but lodge comfortably for a few hours anywhere.

On such a day the man who milks his cow in the street is compelled to lay hold of her tail, for fear of losing sight
15   of her; while the butcher-boy who carries out meat is often minus a joint or two when he reaches the door at which his orders ought to have been delivered. Should such a day be Smithfield market, all the cellar- flaps in the little by-streets are left open, in the hopes of catching a few stray sheep, and having a stock of mutton for nothing; should a prize bullock tumble in, they make no bones of him, but salt down what is left, and bless the fog for supplying them with so much excellent beef.

20   A stranger to London, when the fog sets in at night, and he looks upon it for the first time, fancies his apartments filled with smoke, and begins by throwing open his doors and windows; thus making bad worse, by destroying all the warm air in the rooms. Once take a wrong turning, and you may consider yourself very fortunate if you ever discover the right road again within three hours; for the houses wear a different appearance, and the streets appear to be all at "sixes and sevens."

25   Although a real Londoner looks upon a dense December fog as a common occurrence, and lights up his premises with as little ceremony as he would do at the close of the day, yet, to one unused to such a scene, there is something startling in the appearance of a vast city wrapt in a kind of darkness which seems neither to belong to the day nor the night, at the mid-noon hour, while the gas is burning in the windows of long miles of streets.

In 1933, the writer J.B. Priestley went on a tour of England. In this extract from his book, *English Journey*, he describes Jarrow and Hebburn in the northeast of England. Both towns were suffering from the unemployment and poverty of the Great Depression.

Source 3 English Journey, J.B. Priestley

The most remarkable giant liner in the world is probably the *Mauretania*, for she is nearly thirty years old and is still one of the fastest vessels afloat. Her record, both for speed and safety, is superb. We are proud of her. Now the *Mauretania* was launched at Wallsend, just across the river from Jarrow; and she has lasted longer than Jarrow. She is still alive and throbbing, but Jarrow is dead.

5 As a real town, a piece of urban civilisation, Jarrow can never have been alive. There is easily more comfort and luxury on one deck of the *Mauretania* than there can ever have been at any time in Jarrow, which even at its best, when everybody was working in it, must obviously have been a mean little conglomeration of narrow monotonous streets of stunted and ugly houses, a barracks cynically put together so that shipbuilding workers could get some food and sleep between shifts. Anything – strange as it may seem – appears to have been good enough for the
10 men who could build ships like the *Mauretania*. But in those days, at least they were working.

Now Jarrow is a derelict town. I had seen nothing like it since the war. My guide-book devotes one short sentence to Jarrow: "A busy town (35,590 inhabitants), has large ironworks and shipbuilding yards." It is time this was amended into "an idle and ruined town (35,590 inhabitants, wondering what is to become of them), had large ironworks and can still show what is left of shipbuilding yards."

15 The Venerable Bede spent part of his life in this neighbourhood. He would be astonished at the progress it has made since his time, when the river ran, a clear stream, through a green valley. There is no escape anywhere in Jarrow from its prevailing misery, for it is entirely a working-class town. One little street may be rather more wretched than another, but to the outsider they all look alike.

One out of every two shops appeared to be permanently closed. Wherever we went there were men hanging
20 about, not scores of them but hundreds and thousands of them. The whole town looked as if it had entered a perpetual penniless bleak Sabbath. The men wore the drawn masks of prisoners of war. A stranger from a distant civilisation, observing the condition of the place and its people, would have arrived at once at the conclusion that Jarrow had deeply offended some celestial emperor of the island and was now being punished. He would never believe us if we told him that in theory this town was as good as any other, and that its inhabitants were
25 not criminals but citizens with votes. The only cheerful sight I saw there was a game of Follow-my-leader that was being played by seven small children. But what leader can the rest of them follow?

After a glimpse of the river-front, that is, of tumble-down sheds, rotting piles, coal dust and mud, we landed in Hebburn, where we pursued, in vain, another man we wanted. Hebburn is another completely working-class town. It is built on the same mean proletarian scale as Jarrow. It appeared to be even poorer than its neighbour. You felt
30 that there was nothing in the whole place worth a five-pound note. It looked as much like an ordinary town of that size as a dust-bin looks like a drawing-room. Here again, idle men – and not unemployable casual labourers but skilled men – hung about the streets, waiting for Doomsday.

Answers

Unit 1

Page 3

2 (a) For example:

1. Are the rest of the narrator's family going to be as eccentric as her?

2. Why are they so poor yet they live in a castle?

(b) For example:

1. There are suggestions of the family's eccentricity: the narrator's sister is beautiful but bitter; her parents have chosen to live in poverty in a crumbling castle.

2. The writer withholds key information about the family and the reasons for their situation, focusing instead on a snapshot from their lives, suggesting poverty and eccentricity.

Page 4

1 e.g. At the start of the extract, the narrator reveals her eccentricity and her desire to be a writer. However, when she describes her wider surroundings, we learn about the family home and her sister. By the end of the extract, the narrator returns her focus to her struggle to become a writer.

2 (a) Answers are likely to focus on the narrator's struggle to become a writer, the family's poverty, the narrator's relationship with her sister Rose, and/or Rose's bitterness.

(b) The opening and ending focus on the narrator's desire to be a writer, suggesting that she is more interested in herself than in her surroundings and her family. The lengthy description of the house suggests the scale of the house and emphasises its dilapidation. The very brief description of Rose's beauty and her bitterness and anger at living in "a crumbling ruin surrounded by a sea of mud" is intriguing. This contrasts strongly with the narrator's very different summary of their situation as "romantic", suggesting conflict between the sisters.

(c) The great breadth, but limited depth, of detail in the extract is intended to engage the reader. These intriguing snippets of information effectively manipulate the reader's initial response to the characters, their relationships and setting.

Page 5

1 (a) For example:
A: "a crumbling ruin surrounded by a sea of mud"

B: "I try to see leaves on the trees and the courtyard filled with sunlight"

C: "It is comforting to look away from the windows and towards the kitchen fire".

2 (a) & (b) For example:
The narrator is an eccentric. She writes her journal sitting in the kitchen sink and writes poetry sitting on top of the hen-house.

The narrator is motivated and ambitious in her single-minded determination to be a writer. She is, however, realistic about her abilities, deciding her poetry is "so bad" that she must stop writing it.

The narrator is a romantic idealist, sitting in a sink for "inspiration", trying to imagine "leaves" and "sunlight" in the dreary view from the window, and describing her situation as "romantic... in this strange and lonely house".

Page 6

1 Answers 1, 2 and 4 are correct and would gain 18 marks.

Answers should refer to lines 13 to 18 only, and Answer 3 refers to later lines from the source; in lines 13–19, we are told only that Rose is "very bitter with life".

Page 7

For example:

1 The narrator is a keen writer, sitting in the sink to get the only remaining daylight to write her journal.

2 The narrator thinks being uncomfortable can be inspiring.

3 The narrator is an eccentric, writing poems sitting on top of a hen house.

4 The narrator is critical of her writing ability, describing her poetry as "so bad".

Page 8

Q	English Journey
	Read again the first part of **source 3** from **lines 1 to 10**.
	Choose **four** statements below which are TRUE.
	Shade the boxes of the ones that you think are true
	Choose a maximum of four statements. **(4 marks)**
	A. The *Mauretania* holds the record for being the fastest ship in the world.
	B. The *Mauretania* is a comfortable and luxurious ship.
	C. The *Mauretania* is a very safe ship.
	D. The *Mauretania* was launched in Jarrow.
	E. The writer thinks that the people of Jarrow are stunted and ugly.
	F. The writer thinks that Jarrow was poorly built.
	G. The workers in Jarrow need a lot of food and sleep.
	H. There are few jobs in Jarrow.
A	B, C, F and H are true.

Unit 2

Page 11

① For example:

A. Life in the mine

C. The actions of the trapper's father, reducing his allowance of candles to nothing

D. The trapper softens his bread in the water in the pit

E. The description of the trapper's working day

② For example:

A. Darkness emphasised in shorter sentences; the repeated contrast of candlelight and darkness, highlight the misery of life in the mine.

B. The shocking contrast of the trapper's age and his life and working conditions; the contrast of the food that is not available with the food that is; lengthy multi-clause sentences reflect the lengthy monotony of the working day.

C. The writer compares the father's actions with those of a "kinder" neighbour to suggest the father's cruelty.

D. The sarcasm of the word "luxury"; the phrase "man and beast" suggesting there is little difference in the lives of humans and animals in the mines.

Page 12

① A. P, Q, A.

B. Q, A

C. P, Q

D. Q, A

E. Q, A

② ⓐ All are valid responses.

ⓑ e.g. A, E, C, D, B

ⓒ e.g. (based on the suggested response to 2b: P, Q, A, Q, A, P, Q, Q, A, Q, A): The key point here is to recognise that, while paragraphs of analysis should feature points, evidence and analysis or explanation, the most effective paragraphs of analysis do not follow a rigid and restrictive structure.

Page 13

① For example:

ⓐ Positioned at the start of a new paragraph, it emphasises the sudden shock to the reader and to the child of being woken in the middle of the night.

ⓑ A series of coordinate clauses builds a sequence of shocking details: the time, the shaking, and the fact that his father has already gone to work.

ⓒ The verb "shakes" may suggest the mother has no sympathy for the sleeping child or, perhaps, that this is simply a daily routine.

ⓓ The writer seems to be aiming to shock the reader with the details of the working life of such a young child.

ⓔ Immediately following the description of the sleeping child, the time and manner of the mother waking the child seem all the more shocking.

Page 14

① For example:

- The progression of events over time from unlimited candles to none is described in a very long, multi-clause sentence, reflecting the boy's slow, steady and inevitable descent into total darkness.

- The final emphatic clause in that long sentence emphasises the end result: "the boy has no light of his own".

- The writer contrasts the father with a "kinder" neighbour, suggesting the writer's view that the father is unkind.

Page 16

Q	*The Secret Life of Bees*
	Look in detail at **lines 1 to 7** of the source.
	How does the writer use language here to describe the narrator's thoughts and feelings about the bees? You could include the writer's choice of:
	• words and phrases
	• language features and techniques
	• sentence forms.
	(8 marks)
A	**Language**
	• She describes the bees as "the show", suggesting she finds the experience entertaining.
	• Dramatic image of "split my heart down its seam" suggest the impact the bees have on the narrator.
	Structure
	• The author gives a strange and surprising image of bees positioned at the start of the novel to engage the reader.
	• In each sentence, the writer adds impact by delaying the most surprising, disarming or dramatic idea to the end: "…hummed along my skin… longing build in my chest…. split my heart down its seam…", etc.

Unit 3

Page 19

① All are arguable.

②–④. For example:

A, F: sorrow is denied then acknowledged at the breaking of the doll, suggesting the power of communication to bring emotional awareness.

B, C, E: "the still dark world" of the writer is contrasted with "the warm sunshine" of the outside world and the vibrancy of objects that "quiver with life" once the writer has made her breakthrough in communication.

A, D, E: The writer's positive response to the destruction of her doll is transformed into the "light, hope, joy" of her discovery and contrasted with her "repentance and sorrow".

Page 20

① **a** & **b** e.g. "Living" suggests that the word has brought life to the water and to the world in which the writer lives – and that the word has gained life through the writer's understanding of the connection between the world and language.

e.g. "Awakened" suggests the life the word has brought – and that the writer was unconscious of the world before she made the connection between language and the world it describes.

② **a** e.g. The writer describes her childish pleasure in breaking the doll, without "sorrow or regret". The writer exaggerates the impact in emphasising how she is "keenly delighted" by the violence of "seizing the doll" which she then "dashed... upon the floor."

b e.g. The writer draws attention to the cause of her frustration in describing "the still, dark world in which I lived".

c e.g. In emphasising her disability and her anger, the writer effectively suggests her frustration and so prepares the reader to respond empathetically to the triumphant realisation she reaches at the end of the extract.

Page 21

① **a b** & **c** For example:

B: "That living word awakened my soul, gave it <u>light, hope, joy, set it free!</u>"

D: "Everything had a name, and each name <u>gave birth</u> to a new thought. As we returned to the house every object which I touched seemed to <u>quiver</u> with life."

E: "<u>seizing</u> the new doll, I <u>dashed</u> it upon the floor"

b & **c** e.g. The writer creates a tone of astonishment and surprise in describing her realisation that language describes the world and creates thought. In describing this as a "birth", the writer suggests the life that language creates and her astonishment at it, while the word "quiver" suggests the power and vibrancy that language brings to her world.

Page 22

①

Identifies a pattern of language use	The writer focuses on her sense of smell and touch.
Comments on tone	The writer contrasts the vagueness of her "misty consciousness" and the "mystery of language" with the excited, joyous tone of the "thrill" she feels when language is "revealed" to her.
Focuses on the impact of the writer's language choices on the reader	The writer's language choices could simply suggest her joy; however, it could also strongly suggest the sense of unconsciousness and imprisonment she felt before she was "awakened" and "set free".
Explores a range of meanings and/or responses	The writer creates a mixture of possible responses in the reader from sympathy to elation.

Page 24

Q	*Picturesque Sketches of London Past and Present* Focus your answer on the second half of the source **from line 14 to the end**. How does the writer use language to describe the fog and its effect on life in London? (12 marks)
A	**Words, phrases, language features** • Humorous images highlight the difficulty the fog causes – and how some take advantage of it. • Vivid description of the whole city "wrapt" in fog with "long miles" of gas lights burning in windows **Sentence forms** • Frequent use of semicolons to link ideas in long sentences creates a sense of fast-paced snapshots of city life • The very long final sentence concludes with, and reflects, the "long miles of streets"

Unit 4

Page 27

① & ②

A: a short, rhetorical question engages the reader, inviting consideration

B: a short sentence in which punctuation is used to create a dramatic pause before an emphatic denial.

C: a sentence listing the various demands and networks of social media with a dramatic ending to emphasise the problems of social media.

D: A balanced sentence contrasts image and reality to highlight the pressures of social media

E: a short sentence in which punctuation is used to create a pause before a disturbing conclusion.

F: a rhetorical questions invites the reader to acknowledge their own experience of the pressures of social media

G: a long sentence listing the impact of social media on people's well-being

H: a short sentence adds emphasis to this final, disturbing point.

Page 28

① A. a, c
B. c
C. a
D. a, b
E. b
F. a, b
G. none (although it is a valid point to make)
H. c

② e.g. This is an emphatic short sentence positioned at the end of the article to provide a shocking and disturbing summary of the great dangers of social media for the reader.

Page 29

① The writer recounts her personal experience of online abuse using a short sentence and the emotive adjectives "vile and abusive" to emphasise how disturbing she found it. A dash creates a dramatic pause before the final short clause "and they're still coming", which provides a powerfully shocking end to the sentence.

(2) The writer invites the reader to consider and admit their own experiences of social media using the personal pronoun "we" and by adding a rhetorical question. The emotive noun "turmoil", positioned for emphasis at the end of the sentence, accentuates the pain that negative experiences on social media can cause.

Page 30

Identifies significant sentence forms	She concludes the paragraph with a final, short blunt sentence detailing the quantity of "vile and abusive messages" she has received.
Comments on their effect	Using shorter sentences to add dramatic emphasis to her negative experience ... The shocking nature of this incident is heightened still further with punctuation to create a dramatic pause before revealing that these messages are "still coming".
Comments on their impact on the reader	The structure of this final sentence is entirely aimed at disturbing the reader and encouraging them to recognise the negative impact that social media can have.

Page 32

Q	English Journey
	Focus this part of your answer on the second part of the source **from lines 19 to 32**.
	How does the writer use language to create a powerful impression of Jarrow and Hebburn?
	(12 marks)
A	**Words, phrases, language features**
	• Consistently negative: for example, "perpetual penniless bleak Sabbath" suggests every day is a day of rest; implied comparison with a "dust-bin"
	• Emphasises the impact on the people of Jarrow: "hundreds and thousands of them... the whole town..."
	Sentence forms
	• Frequent use of shorter sentences for dramatic emphasis: "One out of every two shops appeared to be permanently closed."
	• Use of rhetorical question, "But what leader can the rest of them follow?", suggests the hopelessness of the people of Jarrow and the failure of their political leaders

Unit 5

Page 35

(1) a. A, B, D, F, G, H, I

(2) Mrs Creasy's disappearance immediately engages the reader in a mystery.

(3) The narrator's character and family relationships are established.

(4) Mrs Creasy's disappearance is linked with that of the family cat, which never returned.

Page 36

Answers are likely to focus on the mysterious disappearance of Mrs Creasy and the relationship between the narrator and her family. The development of character and relationship is interspersed with an intriguing narrative thread of elements suggesting possible reasons for, and the likely outcome of, Mrs Creasy's disappearance.

Page 37

(1) A. a, d
B: none
C: c, d
D: b, c
E: b, c, d
F: a, d

(2) & (3) Comments A, C, D, E are the most perceptive. Comment B is largely irrelevant. Comment F offers the most limited, ineffective (and clichéd) response.

Page 38

(1) Ideas could include:

• The suggestion of abduction works in conjunction with Mr Creasy's behaviour: is he distressed by his wife's disappearance or the reason for her disappearance? Has he harmed her? These suggestions of possible explanations for her disappearance work to build up intrigue and suspense in the reader.

• The writer creates an immediately appealing, amusing narrator and secondary characters to engage and build a relationship with readers.

Page 40

Q	The Secret Life of Bees
	You now need to think about the whole of the Source.
	This text is from the opening of a novel.
	How has the writer structured the text to interest you as a reader?
	You could write about:
	• what the writer focuses your attention on at the beginning
	• how and why the writer changes this focus as the Source develops
	• any other structural features that interest you.
	(8 marks)

A	• Startling image of bees in the opening engages the reader immediately • Frequent references to dramatic events raise a number of significant questions: "my life went spinning off into a whole new orbit… everything that happened that summer…" • A shocking ending focuses the reader on the relationship between the narrator, her mother and her mother's death: "It was an accident. You didn't mean to do it."

Unit 6

Page 43

2 **a** & **b** For example:

A. Brenda and Freda watch the funeral: Brenda is cynical and disinterested; Freda is moved.

B. Brenda and Freda discuss the funeral: Brenda is unemotional and introverted; Freda enjoys the spectacle of a funeral as a fitting end to a full life.

C. Brenda and Freda's attitudes to the Outing: Brenda expects a miserable, rainy picnic; Freda hopes for romance.

3 Freda is emotional, romantic and idealistic whereas Brenda is introverted, cynical and practical.

Page 44

1 **a** A comic contrast between two very different characters.

b & **c** e.g. "Freda was enjoying herself" suggests she takes pleasure in shows of emotion, despite the fact that, as Brenda cynically points out, she "didn't know her". Brenda is "easily embarrassed" and does not want to be seen "gawping" while Freda is "opulent at the window".

d The writer effectively uses the shared experience of the funeral to develop character and create humour in contrasting Freda's ostentatious show of emotion with Brenda's cynical detachment. For example, while Freda is happy to be seen watching, "opulent at the window", Brenda is "easily embarrassed" and doesn't "care to be seen gawping".

Page 45

1 For example: Freda is happy to "gawp" while Brenda does not wish to be seen.

2 **a** e.g. In A and B the writer contrasts Freda's exaggeratedly emotional response with Brenda's cold cynicism. In C and D the writer again contrasts Freda's idealism with Brenda's realism.

d e.g. The details observed by the characters (and those observed by the narrator) suggest that Brenda's view is closer to the truth and so exaggerates Freda's idealism.

Page 46

1	Identifies the author's intention	At the start of this section of the source, the writer contrasts Brenda and Freda's attitudes to the funeral.
	Analyses the writer's choices	The contrast in Freda and Brenda is emphasised in the use of sentence structure and vocabulary: Freda's dialogue is written in longer, more descriptive sentences while Brenda's is short and blunt…
	Makes a connection between related details/ideas from the text	It is, therefore, not surprising that practical, cynical Brenda expects the Outing to be spoiled by rain while romantic Freda hopes she will be seduced by Vittorio.
	Evaluates the writer's success	The writer creates a clear picture of Brenda's and Freda's very different attitudes and the conflict between them.

Page 48

Q	*The Secret Life of Bees* Focus this part of your answer on the second part of the source, from **line 14 to the end**. A student, having read this section of the text, said: "This part of the text suggests the kind of childhood that the narrator experienced. It makes me ask lots of questions about her life." To what extent do you agree? In your response, you could: • consider your own impressions of the narrator's childhood • evaluate how the writer encourages you to ask questions • support your opinions with quotations from the text. (20 marks)
A	• Intriguing references to the narrator's family relationships prompt the reader to ask questions • e.g. Rosaleen, "I'd been her pet guinea pig" suggesting experimentation or a close relationship • e.g. Suggestions of a distant relationship between the narrator and her father, "who I called T.Ray". • e.g. Sympathy at the death of the narrator's mother when she was four soon turns to shock, "You didn't mean to do it".

Unit 7

Page 51

1 **a** & **b** D and E imply that the discovery was an obvious and poorly executed hoax.

2 The information from both texts describe fraudulent discoveries, although source B clearly states the discovery was a hoax, while source A only implies deception by giving details of the materials from which the skeleton was created.

Selections of key information are likely to focus on:

- Source A: the appearance of the skeleton; the responses of experts to the skeleton; the exhibitor's response to the writer's opinion of the skeleton.

- Source B: details of how the skull was created; the investigators' conclusions on the scale of the hoax and the motives of its perpetrators.

Page 52

① For example:

- Source A: it was nothing more than the skeleton of a young mastodon. ... The cranium was entirely wanting from the lower margin of the orbits, back; but a raw-hide cranium was fitted.

- Source B: artificial abrasion of chimpanzee's teeth... The black coating on the canine tooth turned out to be ... "a tough, flexible paint-like substance."

② ⓐ For example: The article suggests that the fraud is obvious to one "informed in such matters" and therefore casts doubt on the expertise of the "distinguished physicians" who "testified that they were human remains".

ⓑ The article highlights how "skilful" the fraud was, fooling even "distinguished" experts.

ⓒ Both articles refer to "distinguished" experts, however source A implies mockery of them for failing to spot the obvious fraud, while source B suggests that palaeontologists and archaeologists were "victims" of an extremely "skilful" deception.

Page 53

① A. is a valid point of comparison but is not relevant to the question: it focuses on the writers not the discoveries described in the texts.

C is inaccurate: source A does explain how the fraud was carried out.

F is a valid point of comparison but limited in its scope.

B, D and E are valid points of comparison relevant to the question.

② ⓐ All the ideas are valid.

ⓑ For example: A, D, B, E, C, F, G.

Page 54

A. Links information from each text	"Source A describes the impression which the giant skeleton had on the media, which "teemed with accounts of the prodigy" and the impact it might have on an "ignorant spectator", emphasising how strange and terrifying its "half human, half beast-like" appearance and "great, hooked incisive teeth" would be. ...The writer explicitly describes the fraud as "unscrupulous and inexplicable", and so "skilful" that even "distinguished palaeontologists and archaeologists" were "victims" of the deception. There is, however, no suggestion as to why the fraud was perpetrated."

B. Refers to explicit and implied information	"Source A describes the impression which the giant skeleton had on the media, which "teemed with accounts of the prodigy" and the impact it might have on an "ignorant spectator", emphasising how strange and terrifying its "half human, half beast-like" appearance and "great, hooked incisive teeth" would be. ...The writer explicitly describes the fraud as "unscrupulous and inexplicable", and so "skilful" that even "distinguished palaeontologists and archaeologists" were "victims" of the deception. There is, however, no suggestion as to why the fraud was perpetrated."
C. Comments on the implications of implied information	The writer seems to be implying that those who faked the skeleton were relying on people's ignorance and the dramatic appearance of the creature to make them some money.
D. Compares information from the two texts	Source B, however, focuses on the motives of those who perpetrated the fraud of the Piltdown skull, rather than the impact it had, and seems to wonder what those motives might be.

Page 56

Q	*Picturesque Sketches of London Past and Present* and *English Journey*
	You need to refer to **source B** and **source C** for this question.
	Use details from **both** sources. Write a summary of the differences between the writers' experiences of London and Jarrow.
	(8 marks)
A	• Both texts describe difficult situations. Source 2: "The whole city seems covered with a crust"; source 3: "Jarrow is a derelict town".
	• Both texts describe people in difficult situations. Source 2: "wholly choked or completely suffocated"; source 3: "The men wore the drawn masks of prisoners of war."
	• Both texts have lighter moments, although only one in source 3: "The only cheerful sight I saw there was a game of Follow-my-leader"; source 2:" bless the fog for supplying them with so much excellent beef".

Unit 8
Page 59

① ⓐ For example:

- Source A: the writer conveys the threat that the tiger presents to humans.

- Source B: the writer admires the beauty and agility of a pair of goshawks.

ⓑ The writers convey very different relationships between human and animal: one conveys fear and danger while the other conveys amazement and admiration.

For example:
- Source A: violent, threatening, dramatic,
- Source B: admiring, emotional, dramatic.

Page 60

(1) (b) While source A suggests an urgency in subduing and containing wild animals, source B focuses on the freedom of wild animals and the writer's emotional response to it.

(2) **Source A:** the opening and ending frame the description of danger from the tension of its escape to the relief of its containment.

Source B: the opening suggests how lucky the writer is to enjoy this chance encounter; the ending reinforces this, and the birds' almost supernatural speed and agility.

Page 61

(1) For example:
- Source A: threat and danger
- Source B: admiration and drama.

(2) The vocabulary choices in source A highlight the vulnerability of the boy and the drama of the wild animal's attack. The vocabulary choices in source B suggests the precision, agility and drama of the birds in flight.

(3) The writer of source A uses long sentences to create a sense of threat, building from a sequence of fast-paced events – the crash, the escape – and their imminent consequences in a street "full of people". The writer of source B uses short sentences to create snapshots, suggesting the pace and drama of the goshawks' flight.

(4) For example:
- Source B focuses on detailed description of carefully selected, indicative features, such as "the big powder-puff of white undertail feathers, fanned out, with the thick, blunt tail behind it, and that superb bend and curve of the secondaries". Source A gives little description of the tiger's appearance or movement, suggesting only the writer's fear, for example: "brute", "beast", "jaws," "seized", "sneaked".
- Source A describes "three tremendous blows" of a crowbar with emotionless bluntness while the goshawks in source B inspire the writer to a series of highly figurative images: "beautiful concentric chords and distances... like a knife-cut, a smooth calligraphic scrawl."
- Both texts use the possessive "my"; in source A, "my tiger was safe again" suggests ownership and domination; in source B, "my pair of goshawks" suggests the strength of the bond that the writer feels with the birds.

Page 62

(1) For example:

A. identified a significant similarity or difference in the writers' ideas and attitudes	The writer of source A conveys the sense of a battle between man and a dangerous, threatening animal... The writer of source B describes a much more positive encounter with wild animals...

B. supported their ideas with range of evidence from both texts	The tiger is "ferocious", a "brute", and the writer has no shame in hitting the "beast" with a crowbar. The goshawks "soaring" through and "carving" the sky.
C. compared how the writers' choices convey their ideas and attitudes and achieve their intention.	Once subdued, the creature is described as "my tiger", suggesting domination and ownership. The writer of source B also uses the possessive pronoun, describing the birds as "my goshawks", but in this text it suggests, not ownership, but the strong personal bond she feels between human and animal.

(2) This response could be strengthened with a wider range of evidence, perhaps exploring the selection of the detail of the 9-year-old boy in source A to highlight the dangerous threat the tiger presents, and the writer's vocabulary and sentence structure choices in suggesting her admiration of the goshawks in source B.

Page 64

Q	*Picturesque Sketches of London Past and Present* and *English Journey*
	For this question, you need to refer to the **whole of source 2**, together with the **whole of source 3**.
	Compare how the two writers convey their different attitudes to, and experiences of, the places they describe.
	In your answer, you should:
	• compare their different attitudes and experiences
	• compare the methods they use to convey their attitudes and experiences
	• support your ideas with references to both texts. **(16 marks)**
A	• Both writers focus on negative elements of urban life, however source 3 suggests hopelessness. Source 2: "scarcely imagine what it is to grope their way through a downright thorough London fog"; source 3: "narrow, monotonous... stunted... ugly... derelict".
	• Source 2 uses humour: "the man who milks his cow in the street is compelled to lay hold of her tail"; source 3: is relentlessly negative, focusing on the poverty of Jarrow and Hebburn's inhabitants.
	• Both writers consider the viewpoint of outsiders, source 2: "to one unused to such a scene, there is something startling in the appearance of a vast city wrapt in a kind of darkness which seems neither to belong to the day nor the night" suggesting an unnatural beauty. However, source 3 suggests a much greater shock: "A stranger from a distant civilisation... would have arrived at once at the conclusion that Jarrow ... was now being punished."

Unit 9

Page 67

(1) Student B's comment is the most effective, using short embedded quotations to allow closely focused analysis of each of the writer's significant choices.

(2) For example: The writer adds to the reader's sympathy by referring to "the greatest kindness" he is being shown at the hospital, suggesting the sympathy that the hospital staff have for him, and by describing Merrick's response, saying that "he has never before known in his life what quiet and rest were", suggesting his life so far has been one of anxiety and aggravation.

Page 68

(1) (b) All are arguable, however "mistreated", "vulnerable" and "appreciative" are perhaps the most precise.

(2) Student B has condensed the phrases "how Merrick is deformed" to "Merrick's condition", "does give examples of" to "focusing instead on", and "ways in which people have reacted when they have seen him" to "people's reactions to it". The use of nouns ("condition", "reactions") to replace verb phrases is key.

Page 69

(1) (b) Student B's response is more clearly expressed. Student A's links too many ideas in a very long sentence. Student B expresses the same ideas, summarising her key point in the short opening sentence, linking two pieces of evidence in her longer second sentence, and summarising her analysis of its impact in the final, short sentence.

(2) (b) For example: The writer goes to some lengths to create an impression of Merrick as an intelligent and affectionate man. He lists his appreciation of the "quiet and rest" of the hospital, his ability to "read and write", the fact that he is "quiet" and "gentle", and that he carries a portrait of his mother because she was "the only one who was kind to him". This is perhaps the most revealing and sympathetic detail of all.

Page 70

The student has:

- very effectively selected and linked a range of evidence from the entire text
- selected precise vocabulary
- used shorter sentences to make a clear point at the beginning of the paragraph and summarise their analysis at the end.

The student could have:

- incorporated more close analysis of key choices in some quotations; however, this might have resulted in an extremely long, unwieldy sentence, weakening the focus of the analysis.

Published by Pearson Education Limited, 80 Strand, London, WC2R ORL.

www.pearsonschoolsandfecolleges.co.uk

Text © Pearson Education Limited 2017
Produced and typeset by Tech-Set Ltd, Gateshead

The right of David Grant to be identified as author of this work has been asserted by him in accordance with the Copyright, Designs and Patents Act 1988.

First published 2017

20 19 18 17
10 9 8 7 6 5 4 3 2 1

British Library Cataloguing in Publication Data
A catalogue record for this book is available from the British Library

ISBN 978 0435 18321 9

Printed in Italy by Lego S.p.A

We are grateful to the following for permission to reproduce copyright material:

Text
Extract on page 2 from _I Capture the Castle_ New ed., Vintage Classics (Dodie Smith 2004) pp.5–6, From I Capture The Castle by Dodie Smith Published by Bodley Head Reprinted by permission of The Random House Group Limited.; **Article on page 26** from Social media is making us depressed: let's learn to turn it off; Social media is addictive, and like all drugs, it's doing us more harm than good; Janet Street-Porter @The_Real_JSP Friday 8 April 2016. The Independent.; **Extract on page 34** from _The Trouble with Goats and Sheep_ Reprinted by permission of HarperCollins Publishers Ltd © (2016) (Joanna Cannon).; Reprinted with the permission of Scribner, a division of Simon & Schuster, Inc. from THE TROUBLE WITH GOATS AND SHEEP, a Novel by Joanna Cannon. Copyright © 2015 by Joanna Cannon. Originally published in Great Britain in 2015. All rights reserved; **Extract on page 42** from _The Bottle Factory Outing_ Abacus (Beryl Bainbridge 2010), Copyright © Beryl Bainbridge, taken from The Bottle Factory Outing, 1974. Reproduced with the kind permission of Johnson & Alcock Ltd.; **Extract on page** From _H is for Hawk_ by Helen Macdonald Published by Jonathan Cape Reprinted by permission of The Random House Group Limited and Excerpt from H IS FOR HAWK by Helen Macdonald copyright © 2014 by Helen Macdonald. Used by permission of Grove/Atlantic, Inc. Any third party use of this material, outside of this publication, is prohibited.; **Extract on page 73** Excerpt(s) from _THE SECRET LIFE OF BEES_ by Sue Monk Kidd, copyright © 2002 by Sue Monk Kidd Ltd. Used by permission of Viking Books, an imprint of Penguin Publishing Group, a division of Penguin Random House LLC. All rights reserved and THE SECRET LIFE OF BEES, Tinder Press (Sue Monk Kidd, 2003) Headline Publishing Group.; **Extract on page 75** from _English Journey_, Special 75th Anniversary Edition, Great Northern Books Ltd (J. B. Priestley 2009), United Agents on behalf of The Estate of J.B.Priestley.